INDEPENDENCE

A Memoir of Secrets, Discovery & Forgiveness

Deb Landry

Copyright © 2020 by Deb Landry
Edited by: Callie Brennan
Cover Design: Bryson Taylor Inc.
Foreword: Jenny Muscatell, LSW
ISBN 13: 978-0-9983867-8-2
ISBN 10: 9983867-8-2
Library of Congress Control Number 2020939193

Printed in the United States of America

Disclaimer: This book is a memoir. It reflects a present recollection of experiences over time. The events are portrayed to the best of Deb Landry's memory. While all the stories in this book are true, some names, characteristics, events, and identifying details have been changed to protect the privacy of the people involved.

Bryson Taylor Publishing
A division of Bryson Taylor Inc.
BrysonTaylor.com

Dedication

This book is dedicated to
Darrin, Cindy, Dad, Aunt Gloria,
my children and to my seven-year-old self.

Thank you all for walking through
this journey with me.

Contents

	Acknowledgements	vii
	Foreword	ix
	Preface	xi
	Part 1: Secrets	xv
1	The Hollow	1
2	The Silent War	5
3	Baby	11
4	The Bar-L Ranch	15
5	Independence Day	19
6	Stolen Innocence	23
7	The Hatfields and McCoys	43
8	A Cinderella Story	53
9	Bad Girl	55
10	Deeply Rooted	59
11	Hairy Monkey with a Size 8 Shoe	63
12	Photographic Memories	69
13	Babies Having Babies	75
	Part 2: Discovery	87
14	A 25th Anniversary Secret	89
15	Life and Death	97
16	Early Mourning	101
17	Letters of Deception	107
18	The Bully and the Knife	115
19	A True Gentleman	125
20	Trip to the Wonderful Land of Oz	129
21	Labels	141
22	Time Discovers Truths	149
23	Sins of the Mother	155
24	Coined a Thief	159
25	Surprise	163

26	Brotherly Love	173
27	Friends or Minions	181
28	The Insatiable Appetite of the Narcissist	191
29	Adoption: Another Word for Love	195
30	Truth Be Told	201
31	The Blindside	205
32	Spitting Out the Truth	209
33	Grave Secrets	217
34	Finding Cindy	223
35	Family Trees	231
36	The Father	249
	Part 3: Forgiveness	253
37	Independence	255
	Afterword	261
	Author Biography	267

Acknowledgements

Writing a book of this nature was harder than I thought and more rewarding than I could have ever imagined. None of this would have been possible without my best friend, partner, and husband, Darrin Landry. Darrin has stood by me during every struggle and success. For this I am eternally grateful.

A very special acknowledgement to Adam Dubay, LCSW, who has led me through an intimate and soul-nourishing experience of acceptance and discovery. I truly have no idea where I'd be without his professional expertise. Although this period of my life was filled with many ups and downs, I was blessed to find the right person to guide me.

Writing a book about the story of your life is a surreal process. I am forever indebted to Callie Brennan and Jenny Muscatell, LSW, for their editorial help, keen insight, and ongoing support in bringing my story to life. It is because of their efforts and encouragement that I have a legacy to pass on in such a gracious and eloquent manner.

And last but not least, to all the Crossroads kids and family. You have all enabled me to build a program that I am honored to be a part of. Thank you for letting me serve, for being a part of our amazing nonprofit, and for showing up year after year to teach others that our future lies within the precious development of our children and youth.

Foreword

Abuse is real and its effects lasting. For years, as a licensed social worker, I have witnessed children struggle through the rubble of mixed messages. They cling to the good while trying to understand the bad. From a very early age, they yearn to come to terms with an idea that even the best psychologists and philosophers have spent decades trying to untangle; how can the same hands that love, also hurt?

The confusion causes a paralyzing effect that erodes a child's sense of self and obliterates the boundary lines within a family unit. The family functions, but not functionally. An abuser often controls a home with the power of chaos and uncertainty, while those within her clutch tiptoe on eggshells maneuvering their way through an ever-changing set of rules. There is an underlying feeling that something isn't right, but it is coupled with some strange, daily sense of normal. Trust is not established.

Children retreat into their own world of isolation to survive the malignant atmosphere. Living under a perpetual blanket of guilt, shame, and character assassination, they lose confidence in their own thoughts, beliefs, and ideas. They live in a world where their opinions are not heard and feelings are not validated. Non-abusing caregivers unwittingly compound this issue. A child often views a non-abusing caregiver as a source of safety and love—a source of comfort and hope, but when that source does not also provide the basic element of protection, a child's security within the home is not established. The road is further paved for children to believe *they* must be the problem. Somewhere deep within, they suspect that is not the case, but the weight of abuse presses heavy, and they believe it just the same.

Physical separation does not in and of itself escape the grip of abuse. Scars may fade, but the pain is not forgotten, nor are the destructive words that have been spoken. They linger deep and beg for continued control—haunting the longing for self-worth well into adulthood. True freedom comes when the responsibilities that have been unfairly heaped on a child for years, are handed back to their rightful owner—a letting go of the misconception that children are responsible for their parent's behavior.

It is then that a person can begin to heal. It is there, where the self is found, and it is in that moment, a solid foundation is unveiled.

Navigating the journey away from abuse can be complicated. The map isn't always clear and the roads traveled may not be the same, but those who have found their way are a beacon of hope, light, and direction for others still searching.

Author Deb Landry found *herself* at a crossroads. Her growing awareness that something wasn't right led her to freedom—freedom from abuse, freedom to believe in herself, and if you know Deb, freedom to conquer the world. It is no surprise that she co-founded the organization, Crossroads, where she has created programs that promote resilience and growth for teens, youth and young adults both statewide and nationally.

Jenny Muscatell, LSW

Preface

A spider's web is a unique phenomenon, and something I have always related to my peculiar childhood home. The strength of the web-house is remarkable; it survives rain, snowstorms, burning hot sunshine, and even hurricanes, much like any sturdy-built human home. With its well-thought-out design and unique, aesthetically pleasing floor plan, the web-house is a welcoming sight for anyone to enjoy.

However, the host's home is her kingdom and whoever enters will be at the mercy of the queen.

Unfortunately for the victims, the vibrations of their presence precede them, alerting the owner that she has a guest and low and behold, it is too late once the invitation is accepted.

Glued to the web-house, the prey is trapped, compartmentalized, and ensnared. It cannot be saved. It cannot escape.

Most think the prey is trapped or caught by accident, but they are not. They are invited in. The spider purposely sits on the edge of her structure and waits patiently for the shiny silk net to lure in the next promising victim.

Sneaky and deceitful by nature, the narcissistic spider remorselessly lures in her unsuspecting guest. It is now time to devour her victim, tear down and rebuild her empire. Cunning and shrewd, she leaves behind no evidence of her capture, her destruction. This performance plays out again the following day. Same story, different prey.

This is the story of my childhood. I don't intend to flaunt victimization, but only to bear sixty-five years of actual events that have shaped my existence—those I lived, and those I discovered through years of therapy and research. Some stories are told by family members, others are a compilation of letters, photos, diary posts and memories; some mine and some from others close to our family. Out of respect, privacy, and love, the names of most people have been changed.

I managed to escape from the spider's web, but not without lasting scars. I was so entangled that even though I was able to walk away, much of that past was embedded in me and disrupted my future. Over the years, I have allowed my feelings of victimization to fade to acceptance, and eventually forgiveness.

Accepting the past and storing it in a safe place has granted me this clarity: my upbringing and conception was not my fault, nor my destiny, but the foundation in which my life began.

Whether you share a similar experience, or find my story foreign, it is my hope that in reading this book, you may begin to recognize signs of psychological abuse or personality disorders within relationships. With this knowledge, we can therefore be better equipped to help ourselves and others find the support they deserve—especially for our children.

Tranquility took the place of fear once I sought help to understand that what I was experiencing was not healthy family relationships. My past was filled with secrets, lies, and shame—someone else's shame, not mine. I was just a part of the enigma, compensated with emotional abuse from a mother who attempted to frighten, control, and isolate me from the rest of society so no one would ever discover her secrets.

Secrets have a power all their own. Discovering a secret has the power to redefine a life forever. Forgiveness is a conscious and deliberate decision to release feelings of resentment toward another person who has harmed you, regardless of whether or not they actually deserve mercy. Forgiveness does not mean forgetting, nor does it mean condoning the harm and pain. Independence allows one to care for their needs and accept responsibility to move forward with liberation and freedom.

***Independence** is a collection of memories and experiences in my childhood that led to a quest to find the truth.*

I hold a sea of memories and have chosen the ones that best fit in telling the story of my journey from secrets to recovery.

Deb Landry

INDEPENDENCE

Part 1

Secrets

In everybody's life there are hidden chapters which they hope may never be known.

Agatha Holly

1

The Hollow

Standing at the crossroads of Water and Center Street in a small Maine town, my seven-year-old self, gazed up the street two blocks to St. Anne's Catholic Church. The church seemed enormous to me, being one of the larger places of worship in our predominantly French-Canadian Catholic community of four thousand people.

A place I frequented several times a week, St. Anne's was my destination for weekly Sunday mass, as well as Tuesday and Thursday after-school Catechism. On very special occasions, I gathered with Mother Superior and the sisters of the convent to make butterscotch candy in the kitchen. This was just one of many memories I have of St. Anne's.

Oblivious to my surroundings, I stood in the middle of the street, making sure never to look to my left. I was afraid of the short unpaved extension of Water Street that lay there, leading to the center of town. The kids in the neighborhood referred to this overgrown pathway as "The Hollow". Mom warned me to never step foot on its grounds and she did, after all, have a way of invoking fear.

Devoid of road signs or street lights, the only adornment The Hollow could boast of was a mess of over-grown trees, entangled with twelve-foot bamboo and burdock bushes that draped down to murky puddles of mud. Only a single worn-down house hid among the vegetation. All you could see or hear from the house was a barking junkyard dog chained to an old wooden post.

My eyes fixated on the two-story New England style house which sat on the corner one block up—painted white with brilliant red shutters. I didn't know the owners, but my seven-year-old mind was convinced this picture-perfect structure housed a flawless family.

Along the narrow path of The Hollow ran a rocky brook that on any work day would be a rainbow of dyed textile waste and runoff from the mills. Flowing downstream toward the east branch of the Sebasticook River, the brook helped provide the water power needed to run the area's five wool mills—each at least a century old.

With the sound of the babbling brook behind me, I wondered why I was there, trapped in this town—would I need to stay here my entire life? I secretly contemplated what my future would be like when I grew older, and why I had an uncanny feeling of not belonging. Would I get married and live in a house similar to the one on the corner? Would I live here forever?

The Hollow saved walking time to the self-contained Main Street of Dexter, and was not much more than a wide footpath—not conducive for more than one car or truck to pass.

The Main Street was filled with small shops, a hardware store, movie theater, bowling alley, a bakery and my favorite store, Ben Franklin's, a five and dime arts and crafts store. Its knee-high counters were littered with toys and trinkets, candy, and nuts. It was heaven for a young local like me. As it was, even the aroma of Spanish peanuts and cashews roasting in the five and dime was not enough to entice me to enter The Hollow. Forbidden by my mother, I knew better than to break any of her rules or there would be "hell to pay". Not knowing what that might mean, my young imagination could only assume a terrifying and ghastly punishment.

I looked back to the quaint New England home with red shutters, the one I thought would be mine someday, where I could live with my "perfect family". I envisioned what my future in that house would look like: a husband with thick wavy hair and a couple of kids running around while I cooked dinner. We would be the happiest people, just being ourselves.

It was strange to think that was as far as I would ever go—around the corner, up one street, always hovering next to The Hollow. Never entering, never leaving. Something kept telling me there was more to life than this, but it always seemed to lay just beyond my reach.

It wasn't the house, family, or marriage that had me frozen in terror in the middle of the street, but the feeling that my life was not playing out as I had imagined. I was accustomed to the sensation of not belonging—to my family, the town, or to the culture. It was as if I was a misfit puzzle piece that had been dropped into some idyllic family portrait where it didn't belong. It fit, but somehow just never quite right.

My inherent yearning to belong made me an outsider —I wasn't a cohesive part of the picture. Relegated to being an onlooker, I spent my childhood always a few steps removed from the rest of my family, viewing life like a forgotten guest.

At the tender age of seven, I hadn't yet developed the tools necessary to untangle my feelings and thoughts, they were just there. The scattered emotions only created a sort of foggy confusion. At that young age, I didn't know I would have a choice in my life's direction.

I saw no indication that my journey was exactly that — mine. Mine to control, mine to change. All I knew was that I was too frightened, and forbidden, to go left to The Hollow, the hill to the church was too high to climb, and I didn't want to turn right towards home.

At that moment, I had no idea that the feeling of being frozen in thought, without a clue of where to go, would be an everlasting and potent memory.

2

The Silent War

My dad, Leo Wilfred Bolduc, was born and raised in Dexter, Maine. Other than a short stint in the Navy, he lived there his entire life. His parents, Joseph and Marietta Bolduc, were both Canadian citizens who relocated to the area from St. Joseph, Québec, and married in 1921, soon after arriving in the U.S. The Dexter woolen mills were an attractive employment opportunity at the time, and my grandfather was just one of many Canadians who immigrated there for work.

Marietta and Joseph were married less than fifteen years before divorcing, and during that time they had three children. Leo, the youngest of the children, was born in 1929, at a time when his parents' marriage was taking a sharp turn for the worse. According to my mother, Leo was not Joseph's biological son— although there was never any talk or proof of this, with the exception to their obvious physical differences. "But your grandfather did the right thing and brought the boy up. He is a saint," Mom would say.

Raised in a French-Canadian home, Leo did not hear or learn English until he started kindergarten. I remember the stories he told of his school days, describing the difficulties of going to a school where he couldn't speak the language. Not understanding directions or the schedule, he learned to stay quiet and follow the crowd. Once he became comfortable with English, he refused to speak French at all.

Dad was born as a postscript, the youngest of three children and a painful reminder of a failed marriage. Standing 5'7" and 150 pounds, Leo was small in comparison to his 6-foot tall brother, Lawrence. They did not resemble each other, nor did Leo bear any resemblance to his sister, Faye. Although born a towhead, which further distinguished him from the rest of his family, his hair gradually darkened to a gentle brown color in his teen and early adult years. His ocean-blue eyes shone and frequently drew remarks from friends and strangers. I, myself, failed to notice how truly enchanting they were until a friend of mine commented, "Your father has the most beautiful blue eyes. I've never seen that shade of blue, and they sparkle when he smiles." I suppose that's not something you notice as a child, but after that day their intriguing sapphire color captivated me.

A true introvert, Leo was not one to say much about his life, accomplishments, or tribulations. He was a soft-spoken and private man who never minced words. He rarely spoke of his time in the Navy, except for the occasional comments, "I don't eat American cheese because that was all we ate on the ship during the Korean War," or "The Pacific Ocean is so blue, much prettier than the green Atlantic."

Baseball was Leo's life passion since grade school. A New York Yankees fan to the bone, he was teased relentlessly by the Red Sox enthusiasts inhabiting most of the state of Maine. Somehow, that never bothered him. His dream was to play Major League Baseball, and that was the goal which kept him going after he joined the Navy. He tried to enlist at seventeen, as many young men did at the time, but was rejected. At eighteen, he joined the service and was deployed to the South Pacific in 1950 at the start of the Korean conflict. He returned to the U.S. in 1952, just in time for major league tryouts. He made it—to the farm league, that is.

When he found out that he had only made the minor league of the Chicago White Sox, his frustration was so visceral it spurred him to decline the offer entirely, and instead move back home to Maine.

Although reserved and quiet, Leo had a short fuse and little patience. It wasn't often you got to see his stubborn side and temper, but he was a master of communicating whole sermons with a single piercing glance.

Playing in the major leagues was his life dream, and the shock of not achieving it on the first try left his ego bruised and smarting. I sometimes wonder if he ever considered the merits of working his way slowly towards his lifelong goal—but blinded by pride, his short fuse got the best of him. I would often tease him that it was a good thing he didn't take the position, or he would not have come home and met my mother, and I would not have been born.

His dream since childhood crushed, he applied to Farmington State Teachers College to become a physical education teacher. If he couldn't play ball, he was going to teach it.

His application to Farmington State was denied. The shrapnel in his leg from the war and the plate in his ear, a result of frequent infections as a child, made sure of that. Having suffered from frequent ear infections as a child, he was left with lasting after-effects. In the days before antibiotics, infections were often left to fester, and children suffered the consequence of ineffective treatments with burst eardrums and chronic mastoiditis. My dad was one of them.

He was forced to settle for a coaching position in the town league, satisfying his love for the sport. He played intramural baseball, coached little league and umpired local games, and he never missed a professional game, either on the radio or television. His dedication to baseball was admirable, but it couldn't pay the bills. With the war over, Leo was in his early twenties and had no other recourse but to find a job, eventually securing one at Fay & Scott Machine Shop in Dexter. He joined the Army Reserves at a branch in town, and stayed with them for thirty years.

Given his outwardly calm demeanor, one would think that Leo would have found a way to work through the various disappointments and setbacks in his life. Unfortunately, he was an expert at internalizing his feelings and therefore failed to process them in a healthy way. This trait would often manifest itself by way of frequent night terrors, headaches, and hypertension post-war.

In fact, the only talk of the war came from Mom when she recounted the nightmares Leo experienced for several years after he returned from Korea. These subsided somewhat, but they never completely ceased. Mom said he was suffering from shell shock, now called PTSD, or post-traumatic stress disorder. The pain my dad and his comrades went through had many names: shell shock, soldier's heart, combat fatigue, and war neurosis. Countless men continued to experience the horrors of wartime well after they arrived back on friendly soil, but the concept of mental trauma stemming from combat was scarcely recognized until after the Vietnam War, when veterans started advocating for themselves.

While he suffered from PTSD, my dad had no support or acknowledgement of the pain he felt. He did what most veterans at that time did: silently concealed and hid away the pain of war secrets, and hoped it wouldn't haunt him forever.

3

Baby

My mom, Marilyn Roberta Fern Bryson, was born and raised in North Newport, fifteen miles from Dexter, but many more miles away in lifestyle and upbringing. Her father, James Patrick Sr., known to his friends as Pat, was a farmer and logger, and her mother Delia, a homemaker.

Marilyn was the ninth child in a family that was terribly familiar with hard labor and modest living. Both of her parents came from large Irish families with ten and fifteen children, respectively. Life was hard, and they were poor, to say the least. Clothes were shared, as were chores, and the children were raised to do their part. All nine children knew the realities of hard work. They worked from sunup to sundown, cleaning the barn, feeding the animals, haying, cutting and selling wood, tending the garden, and harvesting vegetables. There was rarely a minute of rest, and from a young age, the children learned the merits of manual labor.

No matter the weather, the Bryson kids walked two miles to the school bus each day. My aunts used to say that Marilyn had it better than the rest of them, because by the time she was old enough to contribute, the hard times had slightly improved. When she started attending school, the family was fortunate enough to buy a truck for use around the farm—which saved Marilyn from chilly walks to the bus stop as she entered high school.

Marilyn's parents and siblings gave her the nickname Baby. It stood the test of time, as even some of her nieces and nephews would eventually call her Aunt Baby. For some, it was a term of endearment, but for most, it became a term of mockery. She had many nicknames: Baby from her family, Mim or Mare from her friends, and eventually Doll from Leo.

Although Marilyn was the youngest living child, she did have a younger sister, Deanna, who died at birth. The only child delivered in a hospital, Deanna's birth was by far the most difficult. My grandfather paced the waiting room floors, impatiently awaiting the doctor's update on the prognosis of his wife and unborn child. He saw the doctor approach and watched him pull off his scrub mask. He expected to hear the words, "It's a girl, you can go in now." They never came. The situation was grave and my grandfather suddenly found himself forced into a decision no man would ever want to make. The doctor's heart was heavy. "I can save your wife, or your baby, but not both. I need to know which way to go." In that split second, my grandfather was faced with the pressure of an impossible situation—a situation that no matter the choice, the outcome would grieve at least one life. He shoved down all the fear and hurt and bravely held himself together. He swallowed hard and chose to save his wife. The agonizing pain followed them home to a crib prepared for a new baby, a crib that would lay empty, accentuating the pain of a husband's choice and the vastness of a mother's grief.

My grandmother was left in an inconsolable state. She converted her grief instead to adoration for two-year-old baby Marilyn, doting over her for the rest of her life, oftentimes at the expense of the other children. It is clear that my mother's behavior was, in part, a result of being raised as an overindulged child.

It was no secret that Baby was the favorite of the nine Bryson children. She slept with her mother every night until she married and left home. Co-sleeping was how a family of eleven made do with a four-bedroom house, and that arrangement was normal for the Bryson's.

Mom continued this *tradition* even later in life. Therefore, it was not surprising that she invited overnight guests into her bed after Dad passed away. Although raised to believe this was normal, she knew it was unconventional, yet failed to care that it made anyone feel uncomfortable by the mere suggestion of it. This odd practice was even applied when she would visit me, expecting my husband to sleep in the guest room so she could sleep in my bed with me.

Although she claimed it was normal behavior, I realized it was a power play to divide and conquer, making me choose between my husband and my mother. From their first meeting, my husband, Darrin had set boundaries in their relationship, and this was one way she thought she could assert control.

4

The Bar-L Ranch

The Bar-L Ranch opened as a horse ranch over one hundred years ago, and sat atop a small hill just off Route 7 on the outskirts of Newport, Maine. For over sixty years it was home to a popular dance hall and bottle club, attracting up to five hundred people on any given Saturday night to dance to the music of the local country-western bands. No matter the quality of music, the Bar-L Ranch was always bursting at the seams with people that wanted nothing more than to have a good time after a long, hard week of mill work, logging, and farming.

The Bryson family was no exception to the rule. Every Saturday night from the 1920s to the 1950s, in rain, shine or snow, the entire Bryson family piled into their old forest green Ford pickup and headed to the Bar-L Ranch. Marilyn always sat on her mother's lap, with the younger girls sandwiched in the cab between their parents. The older girls and the three boys huddled in the truck bed with warm coats and scarves to protect the sisters' coiffure. They never fought or argued when they were young. They knew better. The wrath of their father made them toe the line.

The Bryson family loved to sing and dance, knew they were very good at it, and would be the first to tell you. It was the highlight of their week, and one of the few opportunities for the family to be social. It's no surprise that most of the well-loved family stories took place with the Bar-L Ranch as the backdrop.

The family's love for dancing was not limited to Saturday nights. My grandmother, Delia, sewed matching outfits for the six girls, and the family traveled from place to place, singing and dancing for organizations and parties in the hope of making a little extra money—our very own small town, New England Von Trapp family.

For years, family reunions always led to singing and dancing. It quieted the waters, somehow breaking up arguments that stewed for generations. Gertrude, Marilyn's middle sister, played the piano while the others kicked up their heels jitterbugging around the living room. Never were smiles as wide or dance moves as extravagant as when the Bryson family got together.

Marilyn's specialty was tap dancing. Even as a depressive and moody adult, at the mere mention of dancing she would run to the dining room cabinet to fetch her tap shoes. She didn't really care if her audience wanted a show – she danced for you whether you liked it or not.

The Bar-L was where my mother grew up and where my parents met. In May, just before Marilyn graduated from high school, she met Leo at the dance hall one Saturday night and they quickly began dating. Not much, if anything, is known about their courtship and romance with the exception of a few photos in the family album tucked in the spare closet, and notes scribbled on old class photos pledging their love to each other.

They had drastically opposing personalities. Leo's reserved and introverted tendencies were in stark contrast to Marilyn's need for attention and outgoing demeanor.

The messages in her high school yearbook and class photos made it evident that Marilyn was popular, especially with the boys. Notes from classmates made to her and some made to her mother, described Marilyn as a handful for her parents.

Though smitten with Leo, Marilyn was not one to settle down. She continued to date a few local boys she knew from high school behind Leo's back. Still, she favored Leo's quiet, mature disposition. His gentlemanly behavior intrigued her and his sapphire eyes made her blush. He opened her heart to new perspectives and opportunities, and was a calm, responsible influence in her young life. It was clear he would be a supportive, loving husband, who would be a good provider for her and her future family.

When September rolled around, Marilyn enrolled at the same college Leo had applied to, Farmington State Teachers College. She planned to become a high school home economics teacher. However, after a few short days, the bonds of co-dependency pulled strong and Marilyn was crying to come home. It would have been the first time she slept without her mother, and she was desperately homesick for her family and friends. Her father could not stand her pain and easily gave in to her request, driving six hours round trip to pack her up and bring her back to North Newport.

Following her brief toe-dip into secondary education, it wasn't long before Marilyn was back in the saddle and dancing at the Bar L.

5

Independence Day

Marilyn and Leo's courtship that started in late spring of 1953 led to an engagement by early January 1954, and a wedding on January 23rd, a day so cold it made even the hardest of Mainers shiver. Sounds of chattering teeth easily drowned out the St. Anne's wedding bells as they clanged overhead, an ominous warning signaling of what was still to come.

Five and a half months after their wedding, on July 4th, 1954, I was born. It was around 9:00 a.m. on a sunny New England holiday at the small Plummer Memorial Hospital, which sat on the hill directly behind St. Anne's Catholic Church. Although my birth certificate never recorded the time, it was easy for me to remember, as for the next fifty-five years my mother would call me on the minute of my birth to wish me Happy Birthday.

That same morning, Leo was playing in the annual 4th of July baseball game at Crosby Field across town. He was not at the hospital when I was born and arrived several hours later, after the game had finished. Although it was customary at the time, it is still strange to think that in the 1950's, men waited on the outside of labor and delivery rooms while their wives gave birth, only to pass out celebratory cigars when it was all over.

According to Marilyn, she became pregnant on their wedding night in January. When pains of labor surfaced in July, she insisted that Leo participate in his baseball game while she went to the hospital to see what was going on, claiming it was false labor. It was not expected that I would be born that day, so her argument that her husband should enjoy his favorite sport and holiday was easily accepted.

This plan worked out strategically well for Marilyn, as she was spared the trouble of having to explain to her husband of less than six months that he was now the father of a healthy, 7 lb. 11 oz. full term baby girl. No amount of cooking the books could have made that math work.

Still, it is bizarre to me that Leo was so easily convinced to leave his pregnant wife while she went to the hospital by herself. Even if he did believe her story, this was not typical Leo behavior. He was always a loving, attentive husband, and he cherished his wife. Marilyn's fear of him discovering the truth made her a very effective story-weaver, or perhaps Leo's desire to accept her story was so strong that he didn't think, or want, to question it.

The story around my birth was well calculated, and none were the wiser. Sisters and aunts counting on their fingers would conclude that Marilyn was pregnant when she got married – but no one dared discuss it.

Later on the day of my birth, Marilyn's sister Gloria, who was then living in upstate New York with her husband and two small children, received a phone call from her mother announcing that Marilyn had given birth to a baby girl delivered two months early. Mother and baby were doing fine.

Gloria was not present for the nuptials in Maine, as it was the dead of winter and travel with two small children in 1954 was not ideal, so the newlyweds stopped to visit on the way to their winter honeymoon in Niagara Falls. Gloria and her husband, Phillip, didn't know their new brother-in-law well, and this was an ideal time for them to connect as a family and hear about the hastiness of their frosty wedding.

While the new brothers-in-law enjoyed a beer, the sisters prepared dinner together in the kitchen. Marilyn mentioned in passing that her breasts were tender and she was nauseous. Gloria, mother of two and soon to be pregnant with her third child, asked her sister if she could be pregnant. Marilyn's face reddened with fury. "How could you even think such a thing?" she gasped. "You know I was a virgin until my wedding night, it's just all the excitement of the wedding!" She skillfully made her anger known, then quickly changed the subject.

This conversation between sisters was soon forgotten. The fabricated story of my conception was hatched and after the honeymoon, the newlyweds returned home to start their life together.

Leo continued his job at the Fay & Scott Machine Shop where he worked on a lathe machine, making parts for appliances, and Marilyn settled into her new life as a homemaker. They began their life together in a second story apartment on Free Street, only walking distance from the machine shop; an ideal place to start a family.

For a while, things seemed relatively normal, despite my "premature birth". It was not an era in which questions were voiced, and everyone chose to believe Marilyn's story of a healthy seven-pound premature birth. The secret was nestled in a soft-pink receiving blanket, never to be questioned. Well, at least not for about twenty-four years.

6

Stolen Innocence

My fondest childhood memories were those that included my maternal grandparents. They were a rare source of nurturing and the loving, stable adults in my life. With their presence came hugs, attention, consistency, and unconditional love.

James Patrick Bryson Sr. and Florence Delia Lynch Bryson, were Bubba and Nana to me. Nana liked to be called Delia—a middle name we shared. She hated her given name, and only used it for legal purposes. In their care, I felt the primitive love and nurturing I so desperately craved from my mother.

After raising nine children, one would expect a revolving door of visitors frequenting their house. Despite the sky-high number of grandkids, nieces, and nephews, rarely was there another visitor other than myself, except for the occasional cousin to play with on weekends. I spent weeks on end at Nana and Bubba's farm, although these visits were never enough for me. I begged for more opportunity, more carefree moments that I only ever felt in their presence.

Mom generously allowed me time with her parents, and more than once suggested, "If you want her, you should take her." Playing the role of the martyr, Mom claimed that her parents deserved to take me whenever they wanted so they wouldn't be lonely. It was the least she could do to pay them back for being loving parents to her. While all along she was hoping they would take me so she would not be bothered with her transgressions.

Nana and Bubba proudly shared stories of me and my accomplishments, the way parents often do. "Debbie did this", and "Debbie did that". "She is so cute, so smart, so precocious". They laughed at my silly anecdotes and childish behavior.

My grandparents were the ones that made the effort to connect. They drove twenty miles one way in their 1956 red and white Dodge sedan just to come and get me. I remember their car as if I saw it yesterday. It was always spotless inside and shiny on the outside, and the front seat had plenty of room for me to stand between my grandparents. I felt like a princess every time I climbed into the car and stood with my arms stretched out to touch the shoulders of each grandparent. Every few weeks that red. And white car showed up in the driveway to whisk me off to a week of bliss, before I would be returned to my parents' house, and reality.

An old black and white photo captures a moment in time one warm summer day in 1958. Nana snapped a photo of me standing in the front seat of the new car. I was wearing a white silk dress with pin stripes and a wide grin. It was a time of no seat belts—no motor vehicle laws for that matter—and there I stood, right in the front seat between them. I remember it fondly. Bubba told that story many times throughout the years. As we turned into my parents' driveway, I calmly turned to my jolly, gray-haired grandfather and said, "Back to this stinking hole again."

They burst into laughter. "What a statement from a three-year-old. Out of the mouths of babes comes the simple truth," Bubba said as he shook his head and beamed with pride.

Memories are a peculiar thing; at times distant and fuzzy, while others more visceral and gripping. They can tap a well of emotion and heighten senses on even a subconscious level. Some can leave us unsettled, while others bring a sense of happiness and security. The latter creates a lasting warmth that rests deep in the soul, carrying a delicate heart through even the darkest days. My time with Nana and Bubba produced these very moments. I often find my thoughts drifting to those days on the farm.

One morning, I found Bubba napping in his old wooden rocking chair. He was a big man, yet vulnerable to the world around him as he lay there resting his eyes. A jar of Vicks VapoRub sat on the coffee table beside him. The cobalt-blue container was colorful and caught my attention. In a sudden moment of ingenuity, I scooped out gobs of ointment and rubbed it together in my hands, creating a thick paste. I gently applied the goop to his hair, combing it evenly through his pure white locks. My tiny hands and my grandfather's scalp both tingled with menthol, yet he didn't move.

Nana, who was cooking in the kitchen, took in the scene with horror. "Deborah Delia!" she cried. "What are you doing?" Man, I knew I was in trouble now. She never raised her voice at me or used my full name!

Bubba slowly got out of the chair and said, "Delia, that's all right, I wasn't asleep and I knew what she was doing, it's okay."

My grandmother told this story often. Apparently Bubba had quite the temper, and Nana, upon seeing the mess of Vicks was afraid he was going to lose his temper with me.

I was never witness to his notoriously angry side, but I heard stories from my aunts, uncles, cousins, and various others. None from my mother, however. She worshipped her father, and in her eyes, he could do no wrong. I suppose the volatile side of his personality dulled slightly with age, and his joy at having a close relationship with a grandchild softened his hot-tempered edges.

Days on the farm were filled with activity; tagging along with Bubba on minor chores, cooking with Nana, playing outside and sometimes just sitting quietly while my grandfather snored in his wooden rocking chair. (I learned my lesson to let him nap and refrained from the VapoRub hair treatments). They lived in an old-fashioned style farmhouse, made even more rustic with small touches of staged antiques, handmade cabinets painted white, and a 1950's era gray and white dining table made of Formica and chrome, accompanied by matching vinyl chairs. The table was an imposing presence. Several leaf extensions boosted its wingspan impressively, where the family of eleven once convened for meals. Hung over the table was a framed Serenity Prayer positioned directly in the middle of the wall. No matter where my grandmother lived, this prayer in its silver frame always hung above the kitchen table.

The kitchen was the largest room in the house. One wall was adorned with handmade cabinets and shelving, complete with a pulldown breadboard for baking, but it was also used to accommodate all the spices and herbs. A large window hung above the kitchen sink, overlooking the backyard and most of the three-acre garden which fed the family for years.

A giant wood stove filled the opposite wall, and everywhere in between one would find an endless trail of handmade treasures—from crocheted doilies to the granny square afghan draped over the arm of the vintage 19th century Victorian chair. The room was lovely, yet the true beauty lay in the moments shared between family, memories I hold dearly in my heart, such as making biscuits each night for dinner, and early mornings spent baking molasses cookies.

My excitement grew every time I saw Nana drop down the wooden breadboard. I knew that meant she would soon stoop low to scoop me up and lift me to the counter where I could watch her mix the batter. The sweet smell of cinnamon and nutmeg filled the air as I watched her roll the sticky dough and cut it into perfect circles using a recycled vegetable can as a cookie cutter—resourceful indeed. She would sneak me some of the dough on her fingertip, as if my mother was watching and waiting to scold her for it. No one could bake cookies like my grandmother. There was so much love in every bite.

Pat and Delia were a unique couple, in that they got married twice in the same year. They first eloped to New Brunswick, Canada, in October 1914. Soon after returning home, Delia's mother planned another wedding for November 11th, as both sets of parents wished for the marriage to be blessed in a Catholic Church. At the time of their marriage, Delia was nineteen, and Pat was thirty-two.

Just a few months later on March 15th, 1915, Delia gave birth to her first child Anna Louise – the little secret they had been keeping. Over the following years she bore nine more children, and miscarried not one but two sets of twins. My Aunt Louise (who wasn't fond of her first name either) was eighteen years older than my mother. By the time my mother was a toddler, several of her older siblings were already out on their own, either married or enlisted in the military. This created what can only be explained as a sort of "only child" mentality for Marilyn, as by the time she was seven or eight, most of her siblings no longer lived at home.

My paternal grandmother, Marietta Higgins Bolduc Williams, lived in an apartment across town from us with her second husband Bina, who we called Barney. I don't remember much about her, and we didn't visit very often, even though she lived less than a half mile from us. Maybe a visit for Christmas, and occasionally one midsummer, but hardly more than twice a year.

I called Marietta "Memere", the French-Canadian term for grandmother. Memere was short and round, with cropped gray hair, and always seemed to be wearing a house dress and an apron. A real-life Mrs. Claus. She always greeted our arrival on her front porch with big hugs and kisses, and I regret how short and fruitless our visits were. My mother despised Marietta openly and without shame. For years Mom claimed my grandmother stole from our family and our dad. It wasn't uncommon to hear Mom call her names like "whore" and "thief", and this dynamic robbed me from any opportunity to create a relationship with my grandmother.

Marilyn gleefully perpetuated the story of the questionable paternity of Leo's father, and attempted to plant seeds of distrust in me against Memere, on the basis that she didn't love me. I never got that feeling from Memere, which only served as additional proof of my mother's tendency towards diabolical meddling.

My paternal cousins lived only two streets away from us, and due to the proximity, I could watch their time with

Memere from a distance. I envied the time they spent with her. Mom must have noticed, as it didn't take her long to volunteer her poisonous claims. "Memere loves them more than you, you know. She always gets them nicer gifts for Christmas and birthdays. She wants them more than you." Looking back, I know that wasn't true. My cousins visited her more often and naturally developed a closer relationship, but in the heart of a child, Mom's statements were spirit crushing.

In all fairness, Marilyn wasn't a popular character on my father's side. Several members of his family openly disliked her, and my Aunt Faye even forbade Marilyn's name to be mentioned in her presence. I eventually realized this was due to Marilyn's behavior toward Marietta, the matriarch, and my cousin later confirmed this to me.

When my paternal grandparents divorced, Joe, Memere's first husband and Leo's father, moved out of town and started a job as a school custodian in Camden, which happens to be one of the most picturesque towns on the Maine coast. It's one of my favorite places to visit, however by no means due to *his* presence.

When I was young, we would take the two-hour drive south to the coast, always on a Sunday, and only a couple of times a year. Our family of four, which included my little brother Jack, who is three and half years younger than me, would hike to the summit of Mount Battie. It was an easy trail but boasted incomparable views from the peak. When we reached the top, my brother Jack and I would race up the stairs of the stone tower, which stood watch at the mountain's summit since it was built in 1921.

Jack, spunky and athletic by nature, would usually try to beat me to the top. From there, we could see Penobscot Bay and Camden Harbor far below us. The view was breathtaking; the vista is one of the most beautiful views in the world, and its panoramic coastline always made me feel relaxed and calm. I loved sitting alone on the outcropping of summit rocks where I could peer down at lighthouses, windjammers, and seaside mansions.

After our descent, we would walk through the town, usually stopping to eat lunch at the Village Restaurant where I would always order a juicy red hotdog smothered in sweet relish with a side of French fries. I eventually moved to the fried clams and scallops as I developed a taste for them, and can still smell the intoxicating aroma of fried seafood, salted to perfection and the coastal sea breeze that licked at my scallop-filled cheeks. In my mind, this was quite possibly the origin of the phrase "comfort food". Aside from the culinary delights, the Village Restaurant was an adventure all to itself. The walls in each booth were adorned with photos of the 1957 film *Peyton Place*, starring Lana Turner. They were captivating to look at and allowed entry into what seemed to be a faraway world that was somehow still close to home. The production was filmed right there in Camden, and being able to visit made us feel a part of something larger than our small town lives.

Occasionally, we would take a water tour around the harbor in a fishing boat to see the seals, bald eagles, and osprey and stop to shop at a little boutique just at the edge of Main Street, known for its odd name, The Smiling Cow—a third generation family-owned coastal gift shop with trinkets and treasures for any age. The back of the store overlooked the harbor and a hillside park that extended across the street to an outdoor amphitheater, where my brother and I would beg my parents to let us play after shopping.

Surrounded by the rich, native landscape of knotty, twisted elm and maple trees, the park was the perfect setting for my daydreams. Handmade stone walls lined its perimeter, fashioned in the likes of a picturesque fairytale.

I used to fantasize that I was in the Garden of Eden. It was a place I could visit in my imagination, whenever I felt particularly sad or lonely. It is registered as a National Historic Landmark, and will always be one of my favorite places.

My grandfather, Joe, lived in a boarding home where he rented a room from an older widow that lived on the first floor. All the tenants shared a bathroom, and each of them had one small room with a closet. *Pepere* (the French-Canadian term for grandfather) seemed a very boring man, who had a sneaky, untrustworthy air about him. He wore a gray suit or sweater and tie every day he wasn't working. The huge pot belly protruding from his shirt would eventually reveal itself as stomach cancer. The handmade bureau in his bedroom held the only other clue. It was filled with open antacid wrappers and Canadian peppermint candy bags, which he always carried in his pockets to share with children.

Pepere had a knack for making furniture, a craft learned in Canada from his father. He had a small woodworking shop in the boarding home garage, as well as at our house in Dexter, where he made a hope chest for my grandmother Delia. I still don't understand why he made his son's mother-in-law something as sentimental as a hope chest, but she cherished it. She used it to preserve all her handcrafted doilies and fine linens. When she passed away, she left the chest to me. Upon opening it, I found my name written in marker in several places – just in case someone else tried claiming it.

I didn't like Pepere. Quite honestly, my skin crawled with disgust just at the sight of him. Even the mention of his name would send every cell in my body buzzing with apprehension, warning me that danger was near. It was uncomfortable to even be in the same room as him. He made me uneasy, even scared, and I hated when he looked at me. These were sensations I felt even before I knew him to be a child molester.

Visiting him was different from visiting my other grandparents, and driving to visit him was preferable to having him visit our home in Dexter. At his house, I was never left alone. When he came to visit us, that wasn't the case. The true blessing was that he didn't have a car or even a driver's license, so we rarely saw him. When he came to visit us, he would have to ride the Greyhound bus. Thankfully, it wasn't very often, and when he did, I hid in my room.

He was truly a disturbed man. He used to leave the bathroom door open so that anyone walking by could see him showering, naked, or using the toilet. As a young girl, I was once unlucky enough to stumble upon such a situation, walking in on him while he relieved himself. His only reaction was to smile mischievously, before I ran downstairs to the living room to hide behind the chair where my mother sat visiting with her friend. I could feel my heart pounding in my throat, and I prayed he wouldn't come down and find me.

I wasn't that lucky. He slithered down the stairs, smiling sadistically while he looked at me like a bird of prey—acting like we now had a shared secret. It made my stomach sick. My mother, having no knowledge of the event, tried to pull me out from my place of safety and scolded me for interrupting the conversation she had been enjoying from her rocking chair.

"I don't know what is wrong with you, but stop it now and get out of here," she said. I could feel Pepere's eyes following me as I raced back upstairs to my room, where I would hide in fear and embarrassment. I knew it was only a matter of time before his eyes would find me again.

He sought out time to be alone with me under the pretense of loving to "read" to me. These were the moments I dreaded the most. As a child, I didn't understand that I wasn't the only victim of his despicable behavior. I found out, later in life, that other relatives had the same, or similar experiences. Unfortunately, we all seemed to take some involuntary vow of silence.

No one discussed his behavior, and no one made claims against him. It was no different for me as it is for many other children that are victims of sexual abuse. Too young to understand the circumstance, and more often than not, made to believe they were somehow responsible. Like so many others, I learned to blame myself.

My mother's love for Pepere Joe was matched only by her hatred for Marietta. Actually, my mother loved men, period. In her eyes, Pepere was another man in need of care, and therefore, a vessel from which she could receive the attention she so craved. They often cooked together whenever he visited, especially around the holidays when it was time for them to make their annual French Canadian tourtiere pies. He would grind the pork, potatoes, and onions, and she would make the pie crust. They would let it simmer on the kerosene stove while they chatted, sometimes sharing a pot of tea, or singing to Christmas carols.

It took me many years to tell her about the sexual abuse, although I knew it would be useless to mention it. I was well into my fifties when I got the courage to bring it up, and even then it was more accidental than intentional.

My husband and I drove to her house to pick her up for Thanksgiving dinner at my daughter Erica's house. It was snowing lightly and she didn't want to drive, so I offered to pick her up and drive her to and from the dinner. When we arrived, she was not dressed and had no intention of leaving the house, spinning the conversation. "Mom, why are you not dressed and ready to go? Dinner is in a half hour," I said.

Still in her bathrobe and looking as if she had just got out of bed, she firmly stated, "I'm not going."

"Yes but fifteen minutes ago when I called to say I was leaving to pick you up, you said you were ready," I responded.

We were prone to disagreeing and this type of banter, but not arguing. This day was different, and turned into a particularly nasty quarrel when I blurted out the sexual abuse I was subjected to by Joe. True to my instincts, my confession fell on deaf ears, eliciting the invalidating response of, "Well it's not a big deal because he is not your grandfather anyway. Your grandmother was a whore." She then unleashed her decades-old rage into the all-too-familiar checklist of all the ways in which she believed I had wronged her. This was a long list, beginning with the behaviors I had exhibited as a two-year-old. I was baffled by her sudden change of subject and blatant disregard for my vulnerability. "Mom, haven't you ever made a mistake?" I asked. Glassy-eyed, she vacantly peered into space for nearly a minute before returning her gaze to me.

"No, I have not, " she bluntly stated.

I turned, walked to my car, and drove away—it was the only response I could muster. I had been a witness to my mother's compassion to others, but never received it. I knew her to be capable of showing something relating to kindness, but only to those she deemed worthy, someone from whom she could gain something of value. I didn't fall into that category, but I always had a glimmer of hope that one day she would show *me* compassion, or maybe a hint of love I so desperately desired. But I was fooling myself. If there was ever a moment in my life when I needed empathy, kindness or love, it was then. Not even the knowledge of my childhood abuse could elicit a nurturing response from her.

She was incapable of managing her emotions. Lashing out or staring off into the distance were both common reactions for her in times of stress. Later years revealed the depth of her disorder and I wished desperately I had understood them when I was younger.

I never blamed my mother for the sexual abuse and assumed she never knew. From the eyes of a bystander, it would seem that Pepere Joe wished nothing more than to read to his granddaughter, an innocent intention if there ever was one. After years of processing what had happened, I realized blaming my mother for failing to notice or protect me from that predator would only hinder my progress in moving forward. Placing blame on her was hypercritical considering that was her modus operandi. I thought if I told her, maybe the knowledge of my abuse would have elicited the compassion and validation I longed for from her.

Sadly, it wasn't the case. One would expect upon hearing such news that a mother would be wrought with grief, shock, or sympathy—but not Mom. Her patterned behavior—starting with total disregard and ending in redistribution of blame—was so ingrained that not even a daughter's revelation could shake her from it.

I was in my late teens when Pepere died. I drove to his funeral alone. It seemed fitting; alone was exactly how he made me feel as a young girl... helpless and utterly alone.

The two-hour drive gave me time to digest the repulsive memories of the past. I didn't want to fake my sorrow of his passing. I was not sad, just relieved, and maybe a little annoyed that I felt obligated to grace the family with my presence. I knew the routine: I would be silent and nod my head when people extended their condolences. As soon as I could manage, I would make the excuse that I had to leave and get back to my children. This is how family gatherings always went. As if on auto pilot, I found myself parking the car in downtown Camden, by my old Garden of Eden, and wandering over to sit on one of the old stone walls. I stared at the trees with their snake-like knots and twists, and I contemplated skipping the funeral altogether. I wasn't sure I could go through with it. The only tears I would shed would be tears of relief, of finally being assured of my liberation from his horrible gaze—but whether my tears stemmed from sadness or joy, none would be the wiser.

I knew what awaited me at the funeral. My sobbing mother, sadden father, and grieving cousins—many of whom, unbeknownst to me, shared in my pain. Pressing forward, I summoned the strength and walked to the church. It was just as I had predicted. Mom wailed and sobbed, Dad sat stone-faced, alone, and stoic.

I remember nothing more of the funeral, nor the drive home. Pepere Joe was transported from Camden, where he died, to Dexter, where he was buried in a plot at the bottom of a hill, far from the graves of the rest of his family.

No more being afraid or ashamed, no more looking over my shoulder for his wandering eyes. Never again would I have to hide behind my mother's rocking chair. He was gone and the fear he created in me had died with him. If only the memories had also been buried with him. Regardless, I allowed myself a moment to revel in the feeling of weightlessness, finally rid of one monster.

I was ten when Bubba passed away on New Year's Eve. I remember his death in a very different light than Pepere's. I slept in Jack's room that night—per his request—we had a babysitter for the evening and Jack was uneasy. Dad woke us up on New Year's Day to tell us the news together. We were heartbroken. I loved Bubba dearly, and he was the first person close to me to pass away.

In the days following, Mom stayed with Nana for nearly a week after Bubba's passing, while Dad stayed home to care for us. My interactions with Mom during that period were limited, and when I did see her, her grief surpassed anything I could have imagined. She cried for what seemed to be weeks. When Nana would come to visit us, it would be Nana doing the comforting, instead of the other way around. Mom fell into a routine of resting on the sofa during the day and calming herself with Diazepam at night. She was absolutely no help to her family or grieving mother during this time.

I wondered if I would feel like her when my mother or father died someday. I thought to myself, *why am I not as distraught as Mom? She seems even more upset than Nana. Is there something wrong with me?* The odd emptiness I felt in response to Bubba's death was yet another emotion I couldn't explain, because I was never given the tools to process any feelings. This fed my already-pronounced belief that there was something *wrong with me*—a complex my mother fueled with as much disdain and neglect as she could spare. It was her voice that echoed between my ears every time I tried to explain my emotions—"What is wrong with you"?

I remember observing two emotions as a child: extreme happiness or anger. There was no in-between or lessons on how to respond to non-verbal social cues. If the emotion was positive like joy, satisfaction, or excitement, then I learned to overreacted with exhilaration. On the other hand, if I was upset, fearful, sad, disgusted or unpleasantly surprised, the learned behavior was anger. Suppressing my essential emotions undermined my ability to relate clearly to others and myself. Over time this can cause harm to a child psychologically.

Now, when I hear my mother's voice asking, "What is wrong with you"? I replace it with my therapist's voice, saying "Whose voice is that"? It is a reminder to me, and I answer "There is nothing wrong with me."

7

The Hatfields and McCoys

The visits to my grandparent's farm grew less frequent after I started attending kindergarten. Without the reassurance that came with these visits, I became more and more aware of the feeling that I did not fit in. My grandparent's presence had created a sense of stability against my mother's strict influence. Left unchecked, my mother's behavior became a source of great confusion to me during my formative years.

All punishment was equal and did not fit the crime, leaving a sense of "martial law" when it came to the rules my mother enforced on me. I learned early on to do as I was told, and to never disagree or I would get the leather razor strap that visibly hung in the kitchen broom closet.

Most importantly, I learned to never cry. Tears can leave you vulnerable, and exposing a weakness in my house was sure to result in punishment. My mother's ill-reputed response of "if you don't stop crying, I'll give you something to cry for", was never an empty threat. This was the environment that she created for my upbringing, and it was the stage upon which I learned to believe that there was something seriously *wrong* with me and if I didn't behave to her liking, I would be spanked or abandoned.

Life became even more confusing for me as I grew older. I lived in a near-constant tug-of-war, between my gut feelings and the information I was receiving from outside sources: friends, peers, and most potently, my mother. If I wasn't being reprimanded belittled, humiliated or teased, I was being ignored or shamed. There was no pattern and nothing added up. It was as if there was some bizarre set of rules that everyone else knew except for me, and by the time I would start to catch on, the rules would change.

This made it extremely difficult for me to make new friends, or hold on to any existing ones. Growing up in a small town in the sixties, I was provided with an automatic social network of neighborhood kids, and each day we would run out of our respective back doors, and only come home for lunch and dinner. No one asked what we were up to, and we were always under the somewhat watchful eye of the various mothers peeking behind kitchen windows and over garden fences.

In the house directly next to mine lived a family with three sons, the youngest of which—Ben Conner— was in my grade. We played together every day before we started attending kindergarten. Our houses were so close, that neither of us could go outside without the other knowing. One day, while playing between our two houses, we began disputing the custody of an old Bayer Aspirin tin which we had filled with rocks and dirt. Claiming it as his own, Ben snatched it away from me and my ensuing tears gained the attention of both of our mothers. The argument that followed was one that would redefine the relationship between the Conners and the Bolducs. From then on, I was never allowed to play with or speak to Ben Conner again, and a fence was erected between the two houses to ensure there would be no contact. What started as a petty disagreement between two five-year-old kids, quickly escalated into a neighborhood war between two families.

Most wars begin in a similar way. The infamous Hatfield and McCoy feud was originally a dispute over the ownership of a hog—a disagreement that resulted in a dozen deaths on both sides of the family.

The Ottoman War followed an argument between two brothers, disagreeing on who would inherit the throne following their father's death.

It takes very little encouragement for a small dispute to explode into all-out war, and it's a trap that humans are unfortunately susceptible to. Historically, wars are waged between neighbors and within families, leaving collateral damage.

Such was the case of the war on Water Street, between the Bolduc and Conner families. It lasted more than eleven years, and required other community members to choose a side.

Every day, Ben and I would walk to school, one several feet in front of the other, careful to never acknowledge each other's presence. We were the casualties of a war that was bigger than we could have imagined. Even as adults living in the same city, we had no relationship—although cordial, we followed the model our families put in place.

Watching the behavior of the adults involved, specifically my mother, I learned that when someone disagrees with you, the only fitting reaction is to cut them off entirely – whether they were a friend, family member, or total stranger. The connection didn't matter. This was my mother's way of dealing with conflict.

The disagreement between our families was trite and unnecessary, and it was the beginning of a long-lasting pattern; a representation of a larger problem of which I had yet to fully understand.

Without Ben to count on as a friend, I went in search of new friends, finding that I had few to choose from. Many were wary of me and my family after the "tin" incident. I was an outsider now.

I sought out people I thought my mother would approve of. I brought home twin sisters who had recently moved to our neighborhood, taking up residence in a rundown apartment building adjacent to The Hollow.

During their visit Mom was gracious and kind, but the instant they walked out the door she turned on me sharply, demanding, "Why would you bring home that trash? You don't need to be hanging out with those Asian girls. Do you always have to bring home the strays? They don't even come from the good part of town. They live where the poor people live."

Her racist and degrading reaction was confusing at best. First, they lived just five doors down from us. Second, I didn't understand why it mattered that they were Asian or poor. My mother seemed to believe that our family existed in the posh part of town, even though we were just several houses away from where the "poor people" lived and around the corner from The Hollow, with its rainbow stream of muck and abandoned houses. This was one way she led herself to believe we were "better" than others, and somehow upper class.

Regardless, I continued to do my best to find friends that Mom would approve of. Steffi was one of these rare playmates, and one day while having a playdate at her house in the country, she casually informed me, "I really like playing with you Debbie, but your father is a blue-collar worker and my father is white-collar. So, Mom said I can't play with you anymore."

What was that supposed to mean? I thought to myself. If Mom said my friends down the road were trash, and Steffi is saying she can't play with me because I am blue collar, then where does that leave me? I didn't understand what she meant. I only knew it hurt, and chose to take the insult on the chin and keep quiet. It seemed best. I wanted a friend, I wanted a place to belong. My heart sank at the loss of another friend. No matter how hard I tried, I just couldn't seem to get this right.

My longing to be accepted was so strong, but my strength to fight my insecurities was dwindling. As an army of one, it was all I could do to simply survive, never mind take on the world. The world, after all, seemed a bit uncaring. My mind raced as it struggled to grasp the infinitely changing rules and societal classifications, further heaping anxiety upon my shoulders. I didn't yet have the skills to handle it, and reacted in a manner many do—I retreated. It was easier that way. I comforted myself with acceptance. *A sense of belonging is just something I am never going to have,* I thought. I swallowed hard and added one more unwanted label to my toy box of imperfections and shortcomings: blue-collar worker.

My new social assignment of "blue-collar" became a convenient solution for several other friends who used me as a scapegoat whenever one was needed.

Clearly, some of the friends I was choosing weren't working out – so, I found new friends who I knew I could count on beyond a doubt. Every afternoon I walked the two blocks home after school, arriving at 3pm, just in time for *General Hospital,* my new friend, babysitter, and constant distraction. April 1, 1963, was the pilot episode, and that very day my addiction took hold.

I have no recollection of what my mother and brother did during this 30-minute window, nor do I remember what came on after my treasured show wrapped for the day – but I remember the feeling of familiarity at finding myself in an imagined reality and the drama, dealing with domestic relationships frequently characterized by the melodrama and sentimentality.

It provided an outlet for me to lose myself in the fictitious world of Port Charles every day. It didn't dawn on me until the series celebrated its fiftieth anniversary, in 2013, that I had been watching the show for fifty years. *What is wrong with me?* I asked myself incredulously, upon realizing how many hours I must have spent absorbing the plot twists and drama of the show. Yet, it had provided me with the social outlet my mother and peers deprived me of. It gave me a structure from which I could derive some answers of how adult relationships should and shouldn't be, and I learned that secrets and lies jeopardize trust and can damage relationships.

From this series, I also learned the consequences of poor life decisions, and the merits of honesty and kindness. I know how this sounds, and it's sad but true—my life lessons were taught by a soap opera. Now. as an adult, I would still be devastated if ABC ever decided to cancel the show!

As I graduated into middle school, one girl told me her mother would no longer allow us to hang out together. When I asked her why, she responded, "She doesn't like you very much anymore. She thinks you're a bad influence on me."

"Why?" I inquired, confused.

"Well, I've been sneaking out with Johnny and got caught coming in late. I told mom I was with you. So, you can't come over anymore."

Another girl who stole a pair of jeans from the locker room, offered to let me borrow "her" new jeans for a week. "I know how much you want a pair, so you can wear mine," she kindly offered. Blinded by the desire for a pair of jeans, I fell into her trap. Jeans were what everyone was wearing and when I asked for a pair, Mom told me, "You have plenty of clothes and asking for jeans is ungrateful."

As a seamstress, Mom had made a dress for me for every school day in the month. My closet was lined with over twenty cotton Peter Pan collared dresses with buttons down the front, ending at a gathered waist skirt; same style, but different patterns on the cotton material, perfectly ironed and hanging neatly in the closet right outside of my bedroom. This look was complimented by my round toed Stride Rite shoes, ankle socks and hairy legs.

Sewing was Mom's niche. Learning this craft from her mother, she would have made an excellent home economics teacher. When creating a garment, there was no need to spend money on a pattern, she could use a newspaper to create a replica of any outfit and there was never a stitch out of place. If there was, she ripped it out and did it right. When clothes were purchased from a store, which was rare, she would show me how negligent the machines were in the preciseness of the stitching and the importance of backstitching to make sure no seam came undone. Each garment she made or hemmed was to perfection. That was the same for housekeeping and cooking; everything in its place and to perfection.

In the end, I couldn't help but to borrow the blue jeans, seeing it as a friendly gesture from a new friend. However, when I heard the owner had reported them stolen, I realized the position my so-called friend had put me in. Horrified, I washed, folded, and returned the jeans to the locker room bin without telling anyone about it. This was my way of standing up to the bullies – quietly, shamefully, returning their stolen items without anyone the wiser, except for the thief who didn't want to be my friend anymore.

In high school, the library became my friend. In the company of books, I was able to lose myself in yet another alternate reality. By the time I reached high school, I was frothing at the mouth for access to the beautiful, endlessly-stocked library provided for the students. Once, I checked out a book on the life of Lyndon B. Johnson—to read for fun—and was anxious to get home to begin my reading journey. In those days, we dropped our books and bags in the hall before going to lunch, and upon returning to my bag after eating, I discovered the book was missing.

Panicked, I raced to the library, hoping it fell from my bag and someone had returned it , but it wasn't there. My heart sank. The librarian insisted that I would need to pay for the lost book if I didn't find it. My mother was going to be furious at me for having been so careless, but I was at a loss for what to do.

Thankfully, I was notified a couple weeks later that the book had been returned by a senior boy who claimed to have found it in the hallway during lunch period. I confronted both him and the librarian, demanding to know his justification for taking a book from someone else's bag. The boy, coincidently the older brother of "white collar" Steffi, responded sheepishly, "Well, I needed it for a report, so I took it."

I stared at him in awe, not able to comprehend his logic. Looking at the librarian, I inquired, "Doesn't he have to pay? Aren't there any consequences for stealing?"

"Pay for what? The librarian asked. "The book was returned – he just needed it for a report and you were reading for fun."

Standing there, in that library, I was flooded with the realization that financial standing could also dictate the severity of punishment, or, in this case, completely erase it. The white-collar brand managed to wash away the boy's sins, and my argument was brushed away like dust on a book cover. There was no apology from either of them or validation that I was a victim of a thief. I learned that day where my place was in that pecking order. Yet, I still had the safety of books, and the comfort of a quiet library to give me relief.

8

A Cinderella Story

In the early sixties, I underwent a tonsillectomy. I remember being at Plummer Memorial, where I was born. In those days, it was standard to stay in the hospital for a day or two after a minor surgery and I was content to do just that, with one of my aunts as my nurse. I enjoyed the extra attention and being waited on during my stay, and was particularly fond of eating lots of ice cream to soothe my throat.

I vividly remember dreaming under anesthesia and still recall the details of my slumber. It came soon after a grapefruit shaped mask came towards my face and the next thing I knew the operating room became a fairytale. I was Cinderella sitting in my kitchen with all the mice gathering around, singing, dancing and getting ready for the ball. The entire story was played out in my dreams like a movie on a screen. I was so relaxed in my happily ever after with Prince Charming, and was disappointed to wake up.

When I returned home, I was able to spend a couple of days on the sofa eating more ice cream and counting the pressed tin tiles that decorated the living room ceiling. I loved counting the squares that were encased in a different pattern and how they connected to the crown molding. I would imagine that a chandelier hung from the capped center medallion when the house was first built, and people danced around like in my fairytale dream.

It was a great memory, even if it was created by a surgical procedure. I savored those moments. They brought a sense of peace and comfort. What could have been an upsetting experience for some children, proved peaceful for me—good in some ways, but as the saying goes, all good things must come to an end, or when dealing with my mother, a screeching halt. Mom worked all day in her sewing room while I recuperated on the sofa. At the end of one day, she decided to present me with a peculiar gift.

"I have a surprise for you," she boasted, handing me an oddly shaped glass jar. Soaking in what I now assume was formaldehyde were two blobs of skin—my tonsils. Mom had retrieved them for me, asking the doctor permission to save them, and he did. "Surprise, look what I got Dr. Sherman to give to me!" Speechless, I stared at the tightly sealed jar. "I will keep them in the china closet for you to see whenever you want to." And there they stayed for decades. The last time I saw them was when I was in my fifties. Sometime between then and her death, she decided to let them go. I feared I would come across them again if I ever had to clean out her house. The thought made me cringe. Thankfully, I didn't.

9

Bad Girl

On many occasions, Mom would remind me of my "bad" behaviors. She recounted events in a very self-satisfied fashion, in which she could peer down her nose in superiority. Most of her stories were about my younger years between the ages of two and eight. By the time I was nine or ten I had learned it was best to not challenge her. I was that bug in a jar. Being a carefree child, I tried to hop out of the tightly capped jar, until realizing that the lid was my limitation and I didn't jump at all—staying within my safe perimeters.

One of the most memorable stories is when I was eight and we went to Bangor to go school shopping for winter boots and a coat. It was always a big deal to go to the city. We only went a few times a year, and any time we did it was a family event. This particular fifty-mile round trip started off like any other shopping experience. We all jumped into the station wagon and headed out. I'm not sure what the budget was for a new jacket, but when I walked into the girl's department and saw the most gorgeous chocolate colored, faux fur Eskimo Stearns jacket hanging on the end of the rack, I instantly fell in love. It had a zip up front with white rickrack trim around the bottom of the arms and waist. The hood had a white faux fur collar that nuzzled and tickled my face when I tried it on. I had to have it. I clearly remember the big sign that said it was twenty-six dollars.

I don't know if it was too expensive, or what the issue was, but Mom told me I couldn't have it and I began to cry. The tears rolled down my cheeks and wouldn't stop. I knew better not to say anything or I would be in trouble and probably sent to a girl's school. I wasn't sure what that was, but it was a threat I had heard often. I knew the tears were not going to help the situation but there was no controlling them. I was mesmerized by that jacket.

She escorted me to the car with one of her classic lectures, one filled with constant reminders that it was her way or the highway, the assignment of power was hers to keep. "If you don't want what I want you to wear, you will have no coat at all," her words blurted out like a dam bursting open.

I crumbled in the back seat—tears gushing harder. I barely noticed Dad jump out of the car and go back in the store. He returned a few minutes later with the coat. I was dumbfounded, happy to think it might be mine, but nervous about how all of this would unfold.

Dad never said much to Mom, but when he did, he meant business and his tone confirmed that his word was final. He looked at Mom with a fire in his eyes, and with a raised voice he said, "She wanted that coat and she's going to have it."

It felt like a victory, but it came with a price. After time dimmed the event, the storyline changed and Mom ranted on, "Debbie is a spoiled brat, all she has to do is cry and her father gives her whatever she wants. Remember the time you had to have that coat?" It was a tale that lasted well into my adulthood, and Mom never got sick of telling it. "She was such a spoiled brat, and still is, always causing trouble. One time she just HAD to have a coat and she got it, her father ran back into the store just to shut her up." I wore that coat for several years before growing out of it. I even kept it in the closet until I was married. It was a treasure. It reminded me of the time Dad stood up for me.

Mom changed the tone and quality of the story several times throughout the years. The details intensified over time and skewed more toward the outrageous with a detailed focus on the criminal intent I had as a young eight-year-old.

Mom brought it up again and again, but looking back I can see how ridiculous it was in merit and timing. What was her purpose? All it did was remind me that I was a bad person, not realizing it was normal developmental behavior.

After I married Darrin, she graced him with this story on at least two occasions. I never gave it too much thought as it was a way of life, however, in a kind way, Darrin pointed out how preposterous, absurd, and abnormal her behavior was and he was right. He had quickly coined Mom as crazy, yet accepted it for my sake.

I was forty-five the first time she told the story to Darrin. It was Christmas morning; Mom and her then boyfriend, Grampa C came for the holiday. Everything was festive and fun early in the morning when our children, Liam and Quinn, who were four and five, were opening their gifts.

Holiday cheer was in the air with Christmas wrapping flying all over the place. Then the mood changed when it was my turn to open the gift from my husband. A string of Mikimoto white pearls. They were breathtaking, something I had always wanted. As the children sat quietly under the tree playing with their new toys, I admired the strand. Darrin draped them around my neck, and the story began.

"You continue to be a spoiled brat," she said, as she regaled us with the story of the coat, and her mood changed from festive to mean and nasty. I shut her out and can't remember the rest of the chatter as I admired my precious gift. It was a Hallmark moment of truth, with the two of us admiring the pearls, children laughing and Christmas lights flickering. There was a shift in me this time.

I do remember the story being repeated one more time when Darrin surprised me with a trip to Turks and Caicos for our anniversary. Yet again, he directed me to be in the moment and making plans for the trip. He was really good at shutting Mom down.

10

Deeply Rooted

The most effective form of punishment I received was the threat of abandonment – specifically, the threat of being sent away to an all-girls Catholic school in Jackman, Maine. For a threat, it had a high success rate; I was scared straight and paralyzed by the notion of being sent away. As I grew older, I may have warmed to the idea of an escape, however as a child, this idea only created deeply-rooted abandonment issues. I hated going to school, in fear that I would return home to an empty house and a family that was dead and gone. On every family trip, I found myself worried that Mom would leave me in some unfamiliar place and return home without me, while the rest of the family said nothing.

The fear ran deep. I dreaded vacations and time away from home. On one trip to visit Dad's family in Thetford Mines, Québec, I was convinced the real purpose of the trip was to deposit me with a distant relative, where I would be forced to live, forever abandoned. What made things worse was being ridiculed for my fear of being left behind. Only when we were safely home did I finally relax.

By the time I was nine, I was the poster child for fear of abandonment and developed strong symptoms later in life. Signs began to rear their ugly head at a young age. I was a people pleaser, gave too much in non-reciprocating relationships, and I had an inability to trust, pushing others away before they could leave me. This was caused by my own fears and insecurities, behaviors I learned early in my childhood, working hard to receive love, and became hypervigilant to the emotional state of others around me, mainly my mother.

Daily reminders of worthlessness wreaked havoc on my self-esteem. The sense of worthlessness was fueled by the combination of abandonment fear and the poorly defined boundaries placed upon me, and became a foundation for the belief that I was inadequate. With a sense of false beliefs and flawed thinking, I was an easy target for any negative label tossed my way.

When I was in the fifth grade, we were provided with the health curriculum on puberty, which included a movie about reproduction. My mother thought it was important that she was the one to explain this to me within the context of her own beliefs, before the teacher went over the information. I settled myself on the sofa in the family room of our home, facing my mother as she perched on the arm of my father's recliner. Absorbed by Walter Cronkite and the nightly news, Dad took no notice of us. I was excited to have this talk, one that didn't involve hearing all the creative ways my mother would find to insult me. Most one on one conversations with my mother consisted of her predicting how poorly my life would turn out, and I welcomed any discussion in which my inherent faults would not come under scrutiny.

As Mom sat on the arm of the chair, she explained the details of puberty: becoming a woman, what the film would consist of, etc. All was fine, except for the fact that she was gently rubbing the inside of my father's thigh, with a domineering and smug look painted across her face.

"Just so you know," she said, "No man will ever love you as much as your father loves me." And just like that, she dropped the bomb. The trajectory of the conversation, first positive, informative and then topped off with the negativity. It had changed course so rapidly that I thought I'd imagined it. A conversation so crucial to a girl's understanding of how to navigate adulthood had turned into yet another mallet, a tool she could use to beat into me the lessons and belief that I would never deserve love —hers, nor anyone else's. I could have a little but not as much as her. This was a pattern I was learning to accept: first the compliment or positive attention, then the put down or disappointment followed by her pity or gotcha statement.

From my perspective, life didn't seem very promising, especially following this interaction. It seemed as if adulthood was a constant game of ups-and-downs that I would never win; extreme highs followed by immeasurable lows. The excitement of reaching puberty and growing into a full-fledged woman was met with my mother's reminder of my lack of worth. This was the "normal" in which she thrived, dancing from one extreme to the next and leaving emotional confusion and chaos in her wake. She was always dancing – metaphorically, and literally.

11

Hairy Monkey in a Size 8 Shoe

My dad and his family were French Canadian, hailing from Québec with lineage going back to France. Like my maternal side, they were blue-eyed and had light to medium-brown hair.

My maternal relatives were made up of Irish, English, and Scottish descent. My mother had hazel eyes, medium brown hair, and ivory skin – although she claimed to have had black eyes her whole childhood, which apparently changed to hazel before she met my father. This, of course, was her way of justifying my dark eyes, which by the way, never changed color from birth. I, on the other hand, have olive skin, dark brown eyes, and blackish-brown hair.

I was a "hairy little monkey", or so I was told. The changes I experienced during puberty helped, taming and lightening the masses of long, dark hair on my arms, legs and back. My Mediterranean style unibrow was constantly victim to my tweezers as a teen, and eventual electrolysis in my twenties.

Coincidentally, my fair-skinned relative Amelia (on my dad's side), had hirsutism, a predisposition to have an excessive growth of hair, sometimes in random distribution. Although her heritage did not lend her to naturally have copious amounts of hair of any shade, her condition resulted in excessive and long blonde facial hair.

This was likely something she was terribly insecure about, and presumably would not want mentioned. That didn't stop Mom. She was constantly pointing it out to Dad, and finding correlations between her condition and my appearance. "You two are just alike," she would say to us. "Debbie has a hair problem too, just like Amelia." She enjoyed bringing attention to it and harping on the subject, as it was an opportunity to point out an imperfection that could be blamed on Dad's side. Also, it provided a convenient connection, biologically, between him and me, strengthening her claim that he did indeed father me, and distancing herself from any wrongdoing.

Mom always maintained a perfect appearance, not a hair out of place. In her early twenties, she developed a small patch of gray on her right temple. She claimed it turned white when she fell off the back of a pickup truck on the farm and hit her head on a rock. She would always tease it up and spread it out across the front of her forehead, as she loved white hair and couldn't wait for all her hair to turn gray, like her father. She would either curl and style her own hair or go to the salon once a week, where she tittle-tattled with her longtime stylist, Jo-Ellen. The other six days she would douse her hair with Aqua Net, wrap it in toilet paper secured with bobby pins and clip it in place to hold the style until the next week's appointment. Not a sight you would want to run into in the middle of the night!

My hair was thick and heavy, and there was a lot of it – I was never able to tame it to my bidding like Mom did with hers.

When I was around eleven years old, I wanted to have the Cher look. My unruly hair was long, straight, parted in the middle, and hanging in my face—the typical sixties look. Sitting on that same sofa as I did for my puberty talk, my mother tried to convince me to wear my hair pulled back into a tight slick ponytail so it would be out of my face. Every parent has had this conversation with their child, attempting to convince them to dress or look a certain way.

However, when I declined her suggestions for the "modern day" look she wanted, her tone abruptly changed to the tune of "I know better". It was a song I was quite familiar with.

"That's okay," she said. "Just know that if you don't start pulling your hair back, your hairline is going to grow down to the top of your eyebrows, then you'll look even more like a monkey than you do now. Your forehead is already so low it probably won't take long."

She shrugged her shoulders, stood up, and pranced out of the room. My father said nothing, had no facial expression, and stared, transfixed at the television. This time, she'd gotten to me. The smugness of her comments left me empty and worried. What reason did I have to not believe her threat? Why would my mother lead me astray? And there it was again, the monkey reference I heard so many times before. In that moment, I felt like a pesky little animal, with no chance of ever fitting in. In an effort not to embarrass the family and myself with no forehead, I found a new solution—bangs; they would cover up my forehead just in case my mother was right about my hairline.

I didn't hear the typical words one deserves or craves to hear as a young girl: precious, sweet, cute, darling. The dialogue of my childhood was filled with comments like "Why are you always reading"? "Every time I see you, you have a book in your hands, what is wrong with you"? Then, as I got older, "You have the biggest feet for a girl". "You are a two-ton Tony". "Where did you get those clown feet"? "You sound like an elephant when you walk". "You need to lose weight". Too much hair. Forehead too low. Too many books. Feet too big. This last one was particularly offensive to my mom, as she claimed it was "Such a shame we can't share shoes".

Mom wore a size five shoe, and always said, "That is the perfect size for a woman's foot, you know." She was able to distort an inherent, unchangeable fact about my body into something near to a sin. I would have rather someone know how much I weighed, which was about ninety pounds at the time, instead of knowing my shoe size was an eight – I was that ashamed of it.

With my mother's help, I gathered all the information I could about who I was and how much I was worth. The person who was supposed to love me, care for me, and reassure me, was in fact the person perpetuating my insecurities—and this was truly traumatizing. I honestly believed I was a big-headed, big footed, fat hairy monkey-girl with a unibrow, with a weird habit of reading, who would never be loveable. Yet without a better solution, I kept reading and losing myself in the story lines of classics like *Black Beauty*, and reading my mother's *True Romance* Magazines. These resources proved far more informative than the puberty talk.

12

Photographic Memories

The living room of my mother's house was papered with an 18th century Petrouchka design, which would have been elegant in presentation except for its intense red color against the bright white crown molding and decorative Queen Anne's Lace tin ceilings. Laid out like an overcrowded museum gallery, the walls were heavily adorned with photographs of her ancestors. The wall space alone could never provide adequate real estate to hang them all. Each piece of art was carefully arranged in decorative fashion. It was clear the living room housed her favorite collections. Pictures spilled over, some occupying space on the mantle, others cluttering up a repurposed antique table.

It was also where photos of cherished friends and family could be found. My high school graduation photo, along with my bronzed baby shoes, (and tonsils) were placed in the dining room china cabinet, and as time went on, any photos of me or my children were hung in the staircase and upstairs hallway. We never made it to the gallery downstairs, but instead it contained the captured milestones of Jack's existence: his graduation, wedding, and even his stepchildren, but there were none of me or my family.

The living room was reserved for her prized photographs. Over time, I began to understand the code behind her choice of pictures, and the order in which they hung. The hierarchy of the portraits resembled a food chain. Each placement was based on a sequence of events or its influential importance: the children she nannied from the affluent and rich *second family*, the priest, graduation pictures of local teens who hung out at her house and finally the two large portraits of her mother and father watching over their kingdom. Mom graced any house guest to a tour of her trophy case, sharing stories along the way.

The portrait of my grandfather, taken when he was about nineteen, lived in a painted vintage-chic frame, shabby from years of wear. At the bottom, a silver certificate one-dollar bill, wrapped in plastic, was taped to the glass. It was the last dollar, and only memento, left to my mother upon the death of her father. The dollar had been presented to Mom and her siblings at the reading of his will—each child was left only one. The remaining possessions were bequeathed to my grandmother. Mom alleged the silver certificate alone was worth a large sum, but claimed she would never sell it – and made it clear that no one was allowed to touch it. Mom attached deep meaning to the photos, some more so than others. They were truly *worth a thousand words.*

A handful of high school graduation photos of Jack's friends and classmates decorated the antique table, each with a story of despair or triumph. The teenagers often hung out at the house with Jack, innocently enough, as it was a safe place for them to gather after school. Parents viewed this after school activity as a positive environment where their teens could socially be with friends under the guidance of an adult who they trusted.

The photos told one story—a story of unfortunate teens who found solace in the comfort of my mother's compassion— gaining the attention they never found at home. In *her* narrative, she *was* the perfect mother, after all. The truth, on the other hand, was something quite different.

What started as a place to meet up and spend some time with the gang, organically became a confessional. Like a secret affair, Mom's role with Jack's friends shifted to more of a platonic liaison, rather than a parental figure. The teens started visiting alone, or on weekends and evenings and as time went by, the boundaries of supervisory rules blurred. Eventually, Mom the Confidant allowed the kids to do whatever they wanted, whenever they wanted, and with whomever they wanted—so long as it was within the confinement of her web.

It wasn't a scenario uncommon for Mom. She, too, once used her older sister's home as a means to secure her one-night stand with a traveling salesman. Not to mention, hers wasn't an arrangement that didn't offer reciprocity. Jack's friends came to confide in Mom about everything. They shared not only their secrets, but family secrets as they eagerly vented to her sharply attuned ear. They purged their souls while Mom took mental notes of every valuable piece of information she could later use as ammunition. She had a way of holding other people's secrets over their heads or pointing them out in order to take the focus off her own. She believed herself flawless and wished for the world to believe it too.

Appearances were important to my mother. Living in hypocrisy by night and serving as a devout Catholic by day, left Mom thrilled when she was offered a job as a seamstress for the local priest. She didn't stop at those duties, and was honored to take on any additional chores he asked of her.

I was never entirely sure of the nature of those chores, but when I saw the priest's formal headshot added to her art gallery display in the living room, I knew his importance to her was immeasurable. When showing his photo on any of her many tours of the gallery, Mom loved to share snippets and details of their many chats, divulging his inner secrets as if she were the priest and he the confessant.

My mother had a certain reverence for the parish priests, and there were several that held the position over the course of my childhood. Around the time I was eight or nine, she had an enlightening conversation with the serving priest.

When she returned home from her visit she informed me that he had declared my name, Deborah Delia, to be a name that was not biblical. Although, in the Book of Judges, it states that Deborah was a prophet and judge of Israel. In fact, although Deborah is one of the few female prophets mentioned in the Bible, it still was not Catholic approved.

My middle name, Delia, after my grandmother, was nowhere to be found in the Bible. Delia, however, was a nickname for the Christian name Bridget, and the priest suggested my name be changed to De-BOR-ah Bridget to meet a biblical standard. Emphasis on the pronunciation —he said that was important.

Mom agreed. From that day on, I would be called DeBORah Bridget, and Mom would sign all my school records with the new middle name, and inform the school and others of the change, despite the fact that it did not match my legal records. I was bewildered by this change. Who wouldn't be? Eight years of a chosen name was suddenly unacceptable to the point that it required changing? No one else in the family was being assigned a new name, and theirs were not biblical either. Per usual, our family unit went along with the new rule imposed upon our lives, and no one questioned it but me—and even that was only in silence.

This particular priest was one of three I remember from my years of attending St. Anne's. Not only did he change my name, but he would eventually be the one to tell me I was no longer allowed to return to church, and was also the last priest to have his photo added to Mom's gallery. It was in fact removed several years after the name-changing incident, once his tendency towards child molestation became publicly known. Mom claimed people were "out to get him", but she removed his photo just the same and tucked it away in the family album. Whether true or not, Mom didn't want to tarnish her reputation by supporting an accused child predator.

13

Babies Having Babies

I gave birth to my first child when I was fifteen, and my second just 366 days after that. I was a baby, having a baby – although I didn't realize this until much later. The father was an older boy, all of eighteen, who worked for my uncle in a gas station and just graduated high school. He was someone who showed me some attention and love, in the form of sex, of course. I wanted so badly to leave that town, that toxic house, and move away from the family with whom I had no fathomable connection. I had a longing for that idyllic fantasy life I had often read so much about—the happily ever after I had seen watching the old sitcom *Father Knows Best,* which included a loving husband, doting wife, and the proverbial white picket fence. I had the perfect escape plan, or so I told myself. If I could just find someone that could possibly love this hairy, big-footed monkey, that would be my ticket. This was my way of escaping, by running away.

Everyone wants to run away at some point. Kids, teens, even adults, all run away from abuse, violence, divorce, substance abuse, neglect, the list goes on. I was no different. Once, I just started running down the street as fast as I could, thinking I could outrun the reality I'd left in my wake, thinking no one could catch me. Of course, my dad caught up with me in the car, and through the passenger side window convinced me to come home.

I remember how I felt every time I wanted to run, and the times when I *did* run. My reasons for running were usually shame and fear. Shame from feeling that I was horribly flawed, inadequate and insignificant, and fear from the panic that it would never end. I thought that removing myself from the situation would heal the wounds inflicted from years of my mother's manipulations.

I wasn't alone. Between one and three million kids run away each year, many becoming homeless and living on the streets. It took me a long time, well into adulthood, to understand that running was not the best way to solve a problem, and I deserved the chance to stay and stand up for myself.

I was somewhat lucky, as I think back. I didn't run too far, and I ran to shelter, in the form of a husband and a new family of my own. I didn't fall victim to drug use and didn't commit crimes, or live on the streets – I'd say I managed to make the best of a bad situation. I was so young, and had been taught so little, that I had to learn all my skills through instinct and. experience.

By the time I was twelve or thirteen, I no longer confided in my grandmother, or anyone else for that matter. I made decisions blindly, without guidance or consultation. I wonder now: where were the trusted adults, relatives, the mentors and teachers who supposedly had my best interest at heart? Were they there, and I simply didn't notice? I honestly thought I lived in a glass house and they saw everything and didn't care, so why should I?

Two months after my fifteenth birthday, I realized I was pregnant. It wasn't a surprise—subconsciously I wanted to be pregnant. I had ingrained in my mind a dream for a perfect family; a mother and child who would love one another unconditionally. It couldn't be achieved with me in the daughter role, but maybe it could work if I became the mother. I knew I could be happy loving a child and having a child love me.

As I look back on that time in my life, I see the complete folly in my plan. I had no idea what I was doing, and there was no method behind the decisions I made. I didn't know I had a choice, or control over my life – it seemed to me, at the time, that my husband had now taken on my mother's role of calling the shots. You could say that life was simply happening to me, although a more accurate analysis would be that I had no choice. All I knew was that I had to care for and love this child.

Needless to say, it's now obvious that I allowed myself to get pregnant with the hopes of it being an escape route from the sticky web of my family.

When I told my mother the news, her reaction shocked me. Calm, collected, and supportive, her ensuing behavior was only one of maybe four times I ever saw her compassionate side. I figured there had to be a catch. Her only major concern was how my dad was going to handle it. She insisted that she be the one to tell him.

And she did. The mistress of persuasion met her husband in the driveway when he got home from work at 3:30 p.m., and explained the dilemma. I don't know what she said, but I watched his reaction from the dining room window, and could tell by his expression that he was far from pleased.

Dad was clearly angry, and deeply disappointed, although he maintained his composure. Mom was strategic in her choice of using the driveway, and broad daylight, as her stage to reveal the news—it ensured he could not overreact. I was expecting anger, but the one thing I never considered was how hurt he would be. I remember being surprised at how strongly I was affected by his disappointment—I never intended to hurt him. Dad had never directly contributed to my unhappiness, and we always had a relatively strong bond—despite his inability to protect me from his wife's and father's abuse. Most of the ill-treatment happened when he wasn't home. Mom called the shots, and he agreed. Maybe it was easier that way, or most likely she twisted the stories. Maybe he just didn't know anything was going on when he wasn't at home. Most likely he was a pawn in her game and he didn't dare to say anything. He was a bystander and to speak up would make him a victim.

I received plenty of attention from my dad when my mother was not around. However, if she was present, she insisted on monopolizing all attention – she didn't allow for anything else. I could only compare myself to a dog on a chain in the backyard, one that the family couldn't get rid of and couldn't remember why they got the mutt in the first place. I was fed and watered daily, and on rare occasions I was allowed to come inside, but mostly I laid on a spot worn down by my daily pacing and thoughts of escape. In the end, Dad's choice was never to make one. Maybe he knew, instinctively, that I wasn't his biological child, and that made it easier for him to stand by while I suffered.

My family's feelings and reactions to my pregnancy were not my concern, nor were they even on my radar. I created a shift in my life; this was my journey now, and I was finally escaping into the fairytale I had envisioned.

Feelings of relief rushed through my body, it appeared as if the entire world was opening and welcoming me to step inside, or rather, sprint towards my new reality. I had always carried so much shame, like a backpack filled with heavy books. The shame was given to me and I held on to it, along with that list of all my shortcomings. What was the harm in adding another book to my load? I could carry it, and more if necessary, I had plenty of experience. The shame of embarrassing my family rose to the top, and I shouldered the burden like I had my whole life.

The next day, after everyone had calmed down, Mom made an appointment with our priest. "Why are we going to the priest?" I asked. She didn't give an answer. I wanted to look into her eyes and search for clues, but she kept her gaze forward. I followed her quietly—a skill I had mastered to avoid her outbursts—we drove up the hill to the rectory that sat across the street from the church, where we would endure our religious consultation. Dad did not attend.

Mom and I sat across the dark mahogany desk in Father Berube's office, in the gloomy shadow of heavy green drapes that were drawn tightly to conceal us from the outside world. Mom explained my predicament, her voice dripping with shame, and he righteously gave me my penance. Word for word, he said to me, "DeBORah, you will go away to a home for unwed mothers, have the baby, and give it up for adoption if you want to be part of this church." As they discussed my situation, I felt as if I had vanished into those hideous green drapes, invisible and insignificant to their conversation. I remember thinking to myself, *have they forgotten me? I'm sitting right here. I have a say in this matter.*

I was in complete and utter shock of their discussion of my shortcomings. Mom and Father Berube were discussing my body, my future, my choice, as if I was a piece of property. Again, I was relegated to the role of observer. They continued to converse and work out details. When the priest finally turned to me, it was as if he was staring into my soul. Addressing my mother purposefully, he pointed to me with disgust. "Look at her! Everything I am saying is going in one ear and out the other. You will do as I say young lady," he demanded.

For my entire life I had diligently obeyed every command, every demand, but in this moment I had reached my limit. I would not obey, not this time. Fifteen years of pent-up anger overtook me like a freight train. I was sick of being voiceless and unappreciated. As the rage churned deep inside me, I felt my body temperature rise—my blood was boiling and it took everything I had to hold back my underlying emotions. Despite the yearning to scream at the top of my lungs that he was wrong, I quickly composed myself and realized it wouldn't matter. I couldn't change the way he thought, or the fact that my mother had subjected me to this treatment. "You will *not* take my baby from me," I said firmly. I held eye contact until he looked away. I then stood up from my chair and left—not just for the moment or day, I never returned to the Catholic church again. I may never have been able to stand up for myself, but I had to protect my child. I owed her that much.

Still, it was a shock to comprehend that the safe-haven of St. Anne's Church was no longer a sanctuary for me and I was not welcome. Pregnancy, apparently, is enough to strip a young girl of God's good will – at least that's what the priest and my mother led me to believe. I was disgusted and distraught, having this spiritual leader throw my faith back at me in the form of shame and rejection.

The nuns had always taught me about forgiveness, and I had fully expected that a few Hail Mary's would have washed away my sin. Their voices echoed in my head the entire drive home, *was everything they taught me about religion a lie?*

Deeply hurt with my faith fading, I pondered my spiritual self. I didn't need the "Catholic" label to speak with God, nor did I need a priest to tell me how sinful I was, I got an ample amount of that at home. I concluded that I didn't need to be Catholic. I didn't know much about the Protestant religion, but maybe that was a good place to start. My religious upbringing in the Catholic church was one of black and whites; I was taught that other faiths would try to lead me astray, and would never show me the way to heaven. Mom's interpretation of this bible lessons was that Catholic's were the upper class of religions. Therefore, when I was forced to question my place in the church, at first I felt a profound emptiness, anxious and loss of identity. I had always been dedicated to my church—it was a place of comfort, but now it had given me an alternative.

It took five years of distance from organized religion for me to decide that I could return to church, this time as a Protestant. My faith never died during those five years; I was simply waiting for the strength to reach out a hand to a more accepting alternative. When I finally did, I found a welcoming embrace waiting for me, learning that my faith lied within me.

Although my mother didn't entirely agree with the priest, she wasn't happy about my religious adjustment. My pregnancy, religious reassignment, and defiance in the face of the priest all combined into a stew of doubt and fear, making her wonder if she was losing her favorite victim or ridding herself from a daily reminder of her shame. She was starting to realize that she was no longer in control – I had a say now, as did my boyfriend and his family, who were conveniently not Catholic.

Prior to breaking the news to my parents, I had already visited a doctor to confirm the pregnancy. We had also been to a nearby Methodist church to arrange for a proper church wedding and reception. However, once my mother began disputing Catholic vs. Protestant, it was clear that no one was going to allow a Catholic (me) to marry a non-Catholic in any church of any kind. We settled for a Justice of the Peace, and left God out of it.

We were married on January 24, 1970, a day after my parents' sixteenth wedding anniversary, in a tiny living room belonging to the town manager. It was a quick, standard five-minute wedding, and I had made my dress by hand, even sewing a white bow to hold back my hair.

No one from my family attended. Staying home under the pretense of setting up an impromptu reception, they were not present to witness my long-awaited escape. A new chapter of my life was beginning, one in which their role would be much less significant than before.

In retrospect, I realize now that I didn't really make a mistake, as many had led me to believe. I was left to make the best decisions I possibly could, without any guidance or help. My parents set shockingly few boundaries for me; they never should have allowed me to be dating when I was only thirteen, especially with a boy three years older. How can I be blamed for having made a "mistake", when no one had ever bothered to show me right from wrong? I was a child living in an adult world.

Elizabeth was born just a few months after we were married. She was so tiny and precious, with entrancing blue eyes. I don't think I let her out of my arms for a year. I made promises to her I didn't know if I could keep, but I would do my best to keep her safe from the world I knew nothing about.

She was selective with who could hold her: only her father, Aunt Julia and I—which was fine with me. Not long after her birth, my husband found a job in a shoe shop in Portland, so the three of us moved south towards a new life. Well, I suppose it was the four of us—I was already pregnant again.

After we celebrated Elizabeth's first birthday, I went into labor with Baby Erica, and finally was forced to pass Elizabeth off to another set of arms.

Erica was covered in long black hair, with the same blue eyes as her sister, she loved to cuddle and sleep. And just like that, a few months shy of my seventeenth birthday, I was the proud mother of two beautiful daughters.

I couldn't have been happier. I had a purpose now, and was consumed with raising my girls the best I could. I didn't have a clue what I was doing, but was steadfast in my goal to teach them to be the strong, resilient women I knew they would become. Although I had few parenting skills to begin with, I knew one thing to be true: all that a child needs is love and nurturing. I had little else to give, but I knew I could give them that.

Over the next five years, when I should have been thinking about prom, going to college, and the excitement of dating, I was instead changing diapers, preparing family meals, getting my driver's license, and searching for a job. We were happy with our little life, albeit trying at times. Eventually, we moved back to central Maine where my husband had taken a new second shift job, operating the same lathe machine that my father ran during the day.

Having finally obtained all my necessary high school credits, I began taking college classes. My college experience would span over many years and was definitely nontraditional. I was parenting two children, yet by the time the girls were ready to start kindergarten, I had just reached an age old enough to work.

After only one interview, I secured a job as a medical secretary and in the years following, worked my way up the corporate ladder to an administrative and management position. I spent thirty years as a healthcare administrator before starting a medical consulting and educational firm, along with a nonprofit after school youth organization. Childhood forgotten, I had made a new life for myself.

Part 2

Discovery

The greatest challenge in life is discovering who you are. The second greatest is being happy with what you find.

Miles Munroe

14

25th Anniversary Secret

As I grew older, a fact that became abundantly clear was that my mother didn't like me. She blamed me for anything she could manage, and I accepted that as part of life. At a certain point, I stopped trying to understand the reasoning behind her inexplicable behavior. In that way, we were able to live in some kind of peaceful agreement, which was further enabled by us interacting very little, and her having almost no involvement in my or my children's life, one thing my husband and I agreed to monitor. Nevertheless, this peaceful arrangement began to unravel during a celebration for my parents' 25th wedding anniversary.

I was in my twenties when we moved back to central Maine. A few years after my husband started working with my dad, they were forced to go on strike, which meant strike pay—a measly $65.00 per week. It was close to Christmas, and my parent's wedding anniversary was looming—yet money was nonexistent. I was heartbroken that I had no money to buy my parents an anniversary gift. I couldn't even afford to rent a venue or send out invitations.

Being a resourceful person, I called in the troops, including Mom's closest sister, Gertrude. Gertrude "Aunt Bert" was ten years her senior and the middle child in the Bryson family. She was a second mother to Mom and took over the role full-time after my grandmother passed away.

I always referred to her as the captain of Mom's *flying monkeys,* or their relationship mirrored the Looney Tunes cartoon *Spike and Chester.* Aunt Bert always did Mom's bidding and she had no idea what she was doing. There were signs that she didn't always agree with her orders from time to time the anniversary party being one. Yet Mom's manipulations always brought her back in line, and she stayed true blue until the end.

Aunt Bert, neighbors and friends seemed to appear out of the woodwork to help with each tiny detail of the surprise party; coworkers and friends all collaborating to make it a real celebration. I made all the food, the cake, and spent what little money I had on printing invitations. We decided to surprise my parents at their house on a Sunday afternoon. Mom would be arriving home from her job as the activity director at the local nursing facility, and Dad would be returning from his weekend away at the Army Reserve. The timing was perfect.

A half hour or so before my parents were due home, guests started arriving; however the one group of people that did not show were the relatives. Aunt Bert was the only relative that came. Given that my mother had a historically volatile relationship with most of her sisters, this didn't surprise me. Yet I couldn't understand the absence of my dad's family.

The infamous instability of the Bryson sisterhood had never been a secret. Stories and rabid gossip floated between the sisters and perpetuated all kinds of animosity and jealousy. Each sister held a role in the mean girl group. Mom and Myrna led the pack.

As masters of instigation, they could rile a crowd to chaos while slinging gossip at every turn. They established an unfortunate pecking order, acquiring power over those who rarely saw it coming. Louise and Gloria played their targets, Bert was the flying monkey and Phyllis was the silent bystander who moved away from it all to avoid the wrath. Mom and Myrna crafted the most intricate derailments by either fabricating some off-the-wall story or taking one little thread of truth and spinning it into a full blanket of mistrust, skillfully pegging one person against another. When they did tell the truth, it was more of a *crying wolf story* and it was ignored. Fights and gossip could be over anything from who gets to keep a recipe card, to the story of Marilyn at nineteen, showing up at her sister Myrna's house one night asking if she and her *Italian friend* could use the upstairs bedroom.

As the latter story goes, Myrna, (thirteen years Marilyn's senior) consented to the request, then gleefully used the story as gossip to share with the rest of the sisters. As the story circulated between family members, hostilities began to fester. From early childhood, I was told Aunt Myrna (alias Jackie, as she didn't like her name either) was "crazy", and not to believe a word she said. It is interesting and ironic now to think how upset Mom must have been when Myrna relayed the story to their sisters, given that Mom did the same thing to their other sister Phyllis. Phyllis had two daughters, the eldest of whom had been conceived while Phyllis's husband was away in the military. Mom loved to routinely point out this more-than-likely indiscretion on Phyllis's part. Seventy years later my dear cousin Dyna-Kaye, Phyllis's daughter, would find out the truth of her paternity, proving Mom's accusations were correct.

Although she had no problem drawing attention to other people's mistakes, Mom couldn't stand having her own brought to light. Most of the gossip and criticism spread by the sisters turned out to be mostly true. The stories of betrayal were secrets, not gossip. The sisters were always on cloud nine to have one-upped the other; to place themselves in a perceived position of power in the family, even if it meant breaking trust or being deceitful.

Given this history, these petty disputes were responsible for the absence of certain attendees, or so I assumed at the time. The sisters, in-laws, nieces and nephews from both sides of the family were nowhere to be found on that sunny January afternoon. The ignored RSVPs told a story of animosity and lies, and unbeknownst to me, was a story that would begin to unfold during the anniversary party.

The dining room table where we celebrated family holidays was set with the best china, and a three-tiered anniversary cake that I replicated from my parents wedding pictures. Finger foods were decoratively placed on platters with lace doilies, accompanied by tiny tea sandwiches with the crust neatly cut off. A punch bowl filled with pink Kool-Aid, ginger ale and ice, crackled merrily in the corner as neighbors laughed and mingled.

Mom arrived home first. She was surprised—to say the least—and stood speechless in the doorway of the living room before forcing a gracious smile. Dad arrived soon after, mercifully. She rushed to meet him in the foyer and, snatching him by the sleeve of his jacket, dragged him into the den and closed the door behind them.

They remained hidden for only a few minutes before emerging with smiles and laughter on their faces, ready to greet their guests and thank them for coming to celebrate their 25 years together. Little did I know, I was the only relative who whole-heartedly believed it was their 25th.

It was, in fact, their 24th.

While preparing food in the kitchen, I was joined by my Aunt Bert, who whispered to me, "It's okay, honey."

"What's okay?"

"Well, they've actually only been married for twenty-four years, but you didn't know." Looking both ways to make sure no one heard the confession, she quickly moved away in order to not be caught engaging in a conversation with me by her sister. Naturally, I was overcome with confusion. Stunned, I wondered what Aunt Bert could possibly been talking about, and why had she chosen that moment to drop such an obscure, million-dollar hint? She had been working with me for two months planning the party.

Then I got to checking the math, which kept me distracted for the entirety of the party. My mother had always told me I was born a year and a half after their wedding day, which would make my math dead on. I even checked my birth certificate later that evening, to ensure I had counted the years correctly, instantly placing the blame on myself.

And then it hit me. On many occasions, I overheard Aunt Bert referring to me as "poor Debbie". I never understood why, and learned to ignore her whispers. Was it possible she said that because of Mom's secret? Did she think the plans would not go this far? Was she wallowing in guilt or did she feel sorry for the way I was treated by Mom. It was a mystery to me but I was used to the bizarre behaviors of the Bryson women.

Mom's reaction upon arriving at the party was far from joyous, and seemed closer to that of a thief who was caught red-handed. Putting two and two together, I realized I had never actually seen records of my parents' marriage, or any documents stating the year in which they wed. I just believed what I was told for twenty-four years.

Mom *must* have been pregnant when they were married. In order to hide their indiscretion, they doctored the dates and got lucky when no one started asking questions. Little did I know, that was not the whole story regarding my conception, and I would not put it all together for another thirty plus years. My immediate conclusion was that my parents rushed to get married because they were expecting, which made sense, except their continued secrecy was confusing. I further assumed that they were embarrassed and didn't want their parents or family to know the truth, so they agreed to tell the story of an early birth. They had kept the secret for so long and my naivete enabled them to pass it off as the truth. The details of my conception didn't matter much to me, as it affected my life very little. However, I do remember the itching annoyance I felt at my parents blatant hypocrisy, haven given me such grief over my teen pregnancy, yet they had behaved no better.

On many occasions Mom had told me her high school days were the best years of her life; the boys, parties, and Bar L, to name a few highlights. Little was said about her courtship with Dad. Thinking that was sad but true, it clarified the loathing and animosity displaced on me because of her shame and loss of freedom. She was not planning on marriage so soon and her unexpected pregnancy cut her good times short.

This was a turning point, the truth was out—so I thought. I felt myself relaxing from years of built-up tension, with the understanding that I was, in fact, blameless. There was still uncertainty, but I didn't much care; I now had context in which to place my mother's abusive behavior. She felt shame for the nature of my conception and held me responsible.

After the anniversary party, there was a new tale to be told. According to my mother, she and my father ran away and got married several months before the Catholic wedding. No amount of reminding could inspire her to admit the adjustment to her story, and she continued to tell it despite the blatancy of her lie.

At some point, I decided to finally push the issue. "Tell me where and when this wedding occurred, and I will get a copy of the marriage certificate for you."

"You can't do that, there's no record. It was in New York somewhere, and I don't remember the details," she told me.

"It's okay, I just need the date and the state and we will be able to find it," I replied.

She was quick to shut me down with one of her lies. "No, you can't, there was a fire." There was no early wedding, this story belonged to her parents.

15

Life and Death

After a divorce in the early eighties, I returned to southern Maine, where I had lived for the first few years of my first marriage. I ran away again, just like when I got pregnant, this time escaping with a promise to never again put myself in such a vulnerable position. I was twenty-seven, and had exhausted all options to fix a doomed marriage. I knew I had to make a change—fear for my well-being was my new motivation. Sadly, my dream-come-true was more akin to jumping out of the frying pan and into the fire—leaving one difficult situation for another which was much worse. More often than not, running only leads to more running.

That being said, this time I didn't jump as fast as I had in my teens. I put a year of thought into it, and I even sought my mother's advice, though I'm not exactly sure why. We didn't include my father—the parent who could have offered sound, helpful guidance. Mom was, after all, the one that took the lead in any family business and she thought it best not to include him. I needed to get out of an abusive relationship, and I needed help. While asking my mother for assistance was normally something I avoided at all cost, my situation was dire and I felt I had no choice. She listened with seemingly sympathetic ears while I unpacked the details of my abusive marriage. It was reminiscent of the day I told her I was pregnant; the quality of her voice and the warmness of her expressions seemed to promise—a reassuring support I wasn't used to.

Telling her felt settling in a way, like I had made the right choice to seek her help, even if it meant I had to live with her while I got back on my feet. Given my current situation, moving back in with my psychologically abusive mother would have been a welcomed alternative.

We talked for an hour, in what I thought to be a safe interaction. I disclosed every vulnerable detail, unburdening myself of emotions I had carried around for years, letting them unravel into a mess before my mother's feet. The process was exhausting, yet I was met with a strange sense of relief. I had never been able to talk with Mom like this before. It was kind of nice, something I had always longed for. Although one could never quite predict what her reaction would be, given the severity of the situation, I was hopeful this time it would be different, even positive.

Sadly, it wasn't. The years of stress and turmoil spilled out like a dam bursting open, leaving me oddly hollow; I could feel it deep in my bones. Places inside me once consumed with worry were suddenly replaced with a sense of profound emptiness. I was drained—fully exposed and vulnerable, when she turned on a dime and stabbed me with her words. Her voice hardened. "DeBORah, you need to stay. At least until both girls are out of high school, then you can leave," she advised. "What are people going to think if you get divorced? Where are you going to live? Not here! How are you going to support the kids?" On and on she rattled. After a few attempted interjections, I stopped listening. Doing my best to end the conversation, I finally cut in. "I can't physically, or mentally, take it anymore. I am going to go crazy, or worse. It is not a safe environment for me or the girls," I said. My voice was steady and strong, nevertheless her ears were deaf to my rebellion. Shrugging her shoulders, she stood and walked away from her seat at the kitchen table, nonchalantly tossing the last word over her shoulder like a hand grenade. "You will be fine. You are exaggerating, as usual."

I left her house that day with the intention of putting as much distance between her and myself as possible. A few months later, I drove two hours south, leaving my husband and mother in my wake.

For the next thirteen years I would work tirelessly to further my career and raise my daughters to the best of my ability. Those years brought a continued pattern of narcissistic behavior from boyfriends, friends, and bosses that resembled my mother's style. They were attracted to me and I to them—for atypical reasons. I managed these years well, likely due to the fact that I had minimal contact with Mom. Although we were only a two-hour drive away, I was a busy single mother, raising teens and working full time. Without social media to keep us connected, my parents were left to adjust to their empty nest and. I became a distant blip on their radar.

16

Early Mourning

Two years after my divorce and move, Dad passed away suddenly. It was the Saturday morning after Thanksgiving. The girls were with their father and I was at my parents' house. Also visiting for the holiday were my parents' friends Thom and Vee, from Massachusetts, and my brother, Jack—who was out hunting with friends that morning.

We were all sitting down to breakfast, with the usual small talk and familiar smell of brewing coffee, when Dad got up to use the restroom. After several minutes we heard a loud thump.

I called out to him to see if he was all right. Receiving no answer, I rushed to the bathroom door. Knocking, and again hearing no answer, I tried pushing the door open, only to realize that the object barring the door was my father's body lying motionless on the floor.

In sheer panic I wedged myself through the small crack in the door, clambering onto a countertop and repositioning him away from the door. I immediately started administering CPR, although I knew at that moment it was probably too late. His face and neck were an icy-blue color, and I couldn't find a pulse no matter how many times I checked. As tears began to obscure my vision, I blindly continued with CPR until the paramedics arrived, refusing to admit to myself that the most important man in my life was dead beneath my hands.

As if trapped in some out-of-body experience, I watched our Saturday breakfast turn into one of the most traumatic experiences of my adult life. My mother was naturally beside herself, hysterical, and was of absolutely no help whatsoever. Languishing in the foyer under Vee's concerned arms, she could not offer support to her daughter or husband; she was paralyzed. I did my best to keep every compression and every breath consistent, something I had no problem doing when I was the health officer in our town several years prior. I was certified in life support, and had taught countless classes on emergency resuscitation – but none of that matters when you're trying to breathe life into your father, knowing full well he is already gone.

I couldn't bring him back, nor could the paramedic crew, all volunteers, showing up at staggered intervals in their respective vehicles. (This was rural Maine in the early eighties, and resources were thin). The first medic to arrive took one look at my father, and said to me, "He's dead, you can stop now."

I heard Mom screaming uncontrollably, and I, on my knees with my back to him, had to resist the urge to jump up and shake some professionalism into his arrogant brain. My head turned like Linda Blair in *The Exorcist* and I snapped at him, "You are not a physician, and your job is to help me get him to a hospital!"

By this time, several other volunteers had arrived and jumped in to put Dad on a gurney and get him on oxygen. We followed the ambulance to the hospital, but Dad was pronounced dead soon after we arrived at the ER. Whether it was a massive heart attack or equally fatal stroke, we'll never know; we didn't seek confirmation. Dad was gone, and no tests could have softened the blow.

For many years, I pondered how this could happen to a young, fit man of fifty-four. Then again, he really wasn't that fit after all. I began to remember complaints of severe frequent headaches, hypertension, and he insisted on smoking unfiltered cigarettes. One night, he fainted in the upstairs hallway and hit the ground so hard he ripped a large gash open on his forehead.

Refusing to go to the doctor, he chalked it up to low blood sugar. Wouldn't you know, several weeks later when he caved and saw a physician, he left with a diagnosis of adult onset of diabetes and high blood pressure. When he told me about his condition, he came to my house and insisted we take a walk out into the pasture behind my farmhouse. There was a lone apple tree that stood starkly in the field, and it was there that he insisted I keep his diagnosis a secret. Pride cometh before the fall, I learned quickly.

My father's poor health meant that by the time I was forty-five, my doctors were already recommending preventative measures for myself and Jack as well. A daily baby aspirin and annual exams were now part of my routine for healthy heart care.

The days and weeks after Dad's passing were harrowing for Mom, Jack, and myself. We went through the motions of making funeral arrangements, trying to respect the wishes of what he might have wanted—but with little guidance, as he'd left no instructions or a will. Our family was entangled in an emotional web of grief. Although I was familiar with the feelings associated with losing a grandparent, nothing had prepared me for losing a parent. I was twenty-eight and there had been no warning, no sign or indication that I should ready myself for such a loss.

As people do, the three of us took our own role in the process. I had little time to process my own grief, as I had taken on the responsibilities of caring for Mom. She was distraught beyond words, and had lost all capabilities for basic functioning. She took the role of grieving widow quite seriously and, I admit, we kept her heavily medicated for most of the first week of mourning.

Mom insisted on having Dad's body brought to the house, following the nineteenth-century tradition of viewing the dead in their home before burial. Respecting her wishes, the funeral home staff removed the window and slid the casket into the house where Dad rested, briefly, in our dining room-turned-funeral-parlor.

Flowers and food were delivered over the course of the next several days, filling the house with the sickly-sweet aromas of lilies, roses, and carnations. The kitchen was inundated with comfort foods: casseroles, cheese platters, deviled eggs and every kind of dessert you could think of.

For three days our friends, neighbors, and family members flooded through to view the body, which had been placed kitty-corner where the dining table usually sat. The sheer number of visitors was mind boggling; the house seemed to be overrun with those wishing to pay respect. From his years playing baseball, serving in the Army Reserve, and having had an abundance of friends and coworkers who loved him, Dad had no shortage of mourners.

Each night after the visitors left, Mom would drag the recliner up next to Dad, where she would sleep with one hand draped inside the casket. I still grappled with whether I felt more sympathy, or pity, for her in that moment, as I watched her warm hand entwine around his cold fingers.

Aunt Bert stayed at our house during that week, and on the first day of viewings my Aunt Gloria arrived to pay her respects. Watching her sister walk up the driveway toward the house, my mother's already fragile composure unraveled before my eyes. "Get her out of here, she doesn't care, she's glad he's dead! Debbie! You have to get her out of here!" Screaming and crying hysterically, Mom would have none of it. Always the dutiful daughter, I reluctantly honored my mother's request. I met my aunt in the driveway and I attempted to explain the situation, receiving a stunned silence in return. Very few words were exchanged, and she turned to leave within minutes. To this day I wish I could have listened to my judgement instead of my mother's hysteria, and used that moment to bring the family together. If only I had recognized that moment for the opportunity it was, instead of deepening the chasm of familial discord. My father's death could have been a time to mend fences, untangle misunderstandings, and bring a broken family a little closer together in a normal family, but we were far from a normal, loving family.

After the funeral, when the house was free of people, Mom took the opportunity to sling an accusation at me. "Someone went into my bedroom and stole a bag of Kennedy half dollars from my bureau. You allowed people to run rampant through the house," she scolded.

Even in the wake of her husband's burial, she found it appropriate to alienate family and start naming thieves. After twenty-eight years of her antics, I had nothing left in me to feign surprise.

17

Letters of Deception

I met my husband Darrin when I was thirty-seven, while working as a healthcare administrator for a group of obstetricians-gynecologists in a neighboring city.

He was working as a surgical technician and ophthalmic photographer for an ophthalmology practice at the same hospital. I will never forget the first time I saw him, wearing blue scrubs and sitting in the hospital cafeteria, sneaking in a quick lunch between surgeries. It was instant and magnetic—so much so, I could practically feel myself drifting towards him from across the room. It only took a few more meetings, at this social gathering or that charitable event, before we were soon officially dating.

At that point in my life, I had developed a pretty clear idea of what I wanted from a life partner. I remember the day I laid it all out for him. I listed my conditions and was clear with my expectations, complete with a checklist. I still can't believe he didn't turn tail and sprint down the road, never to look back. Evidently, he understood me – more than I understood myself. He wasn't scared by the tough, uncompromising woman before him; in fact he respected me for it.

From the total pushover I had been as an adolescent, in my thirties I was decidedly on the opposite end of the spectrum; never budging, resolute, demanding of the treatment I deserved. Darrin never flinched, and instead became my partner for life.

Thirty years later, we still stand side-by-side through all of life's ups and downs. Life partners as well as business partners, he is truly the love of my life. Although he may not fully understand the intensity of my upbringing and early years, he has always supported me and listened to my stories, without judgement.

When it came time to introduce him to my mother, I was more than a little trepidatious. He had heard many stories of my mother's behavior, and I did my best to prepare him. Finally, five months into our relationship, I bit the bullet and introduced them at Easter dinner. Truth be told, I locked the doors of our home when she arrived so he couldn't run away.

Mom arrived early that Sunday morning, her famous coffee cake in hand, followed by her "boyfriend at the time". Marching through the front door, she passed me by like an old door stop and made a beeline for Darrin.

"Hi, I'm Marilyn, you can call me Nana," she announced.

In return, Darrin replied, "I have two grandmothers, I'll just call you Marilyn."

I will never forget the look of utter shock on her face—it took all I had to refrain from bursting out laughing. Mom, however, was not impressed. Casting off her net and missing him entirely sent her into a tailspin that set Darrin up to be a victim for revenge and set the tone for their entire relationship. She was not accustomed to rejection and saw this as being the subject of public humiliation. Yet Darrin took the upper hand in the relationship—a newly established pecking order, one she would not tolerate over the years.

My brother Jack and daughter Erica joined us for Easter dinner, and early in the afternoon I had to drive Erica back to Boston where she was attending college. Packing up, she said, "Can I take some of this coffee cake back with me?"

Whether consciously or not, Jack loved to play games with Mom. He could put her in a downward spiral in a blink of an eye, and she in turn wanted to do anything and everything he asked.

"Wait, I want the cake," Jack said with a smile. "And I don't like the edges."

Mom, taking what remained of the sheet cake (almost all of it), carefully cut one-inch squares around the perimeter of the cookie sheet, removed each piece, and proceeded to pack them in tinfoil for Erica to take back to college. The inside of the cake was then wrapped and given to Jack. A Nana-ism that is still talked about to this day, this story is only one of many depicting Mom's tendency towards favoritism.

On Christmas Eve that same year, Darrin asked me to marry him. The girls were home from college, and in on Darrin's plan. They conveniently left the house for a couple of hours, so that he could get down on one knee and propose by the Christmas tree. As a family, we planned for a May wedding, with a honeymoon in Italy.

Everything was blissful and romantic until a few weeks before the wedding when I received Mom's Letter. The Letter became a prerequisite to any major event in our family; it was the spoiler, the surprise that usually came in verbal format. Just like any major discussion I had with her as a child, all would be going as expected until she sprung her surprise nasty ending. Big life-changing events were no different.

A multipage, handwritten, insidious letter scribbled on lined white stationary arrived in the mail from Mom, informing me of what a huge mistake I was about to make. She described, in detail, her belief that I did not deserve this marriage, as I had been wed before and I would be arrogant to think that this attempt would end up any different, or any better, than my first. She claimed I was a disgrace to the family, a failure, and nothing else would come of the marriage to a younger man, other than more failure and embarrassment. With a reminder that no one would ever love me, she ended the letter citing her list of grievances she had held against me since I was a child , and again reminding me why this marriage could never last.

Although I had grown accustomed to her perpetual sabotage, this letter exposed her devious narcissistic nature in such a way that made the words even more damaging. The intensity of The Letter signified her desperate attempt to move from hidden abuse to more aggressive actions, grasping for the control she thought she was losing. I felt vulnerable, insecure, and began to doubt whether I truly deserved the happiness I had found with Darrin. I was being pulled back into the psychological abuse I experienced as a child, weakening my resolve and making it easy to fall victim to her manipulations. The Letter was Mom's last-ditch effort to take back some control over me, discredit Darrin, and it nearly worked. I thought the years of distance from her would have cured me of my vulnerability, but it had merely been dormant. The Letter reminded me of the suffering she caused me, and that I still had a long way to go in healing myself from her abuse. I had not made the progress I thought in the relationship. My normal state of health, mind, and strength were weakened by her interference. At first I didn't show The Letter to Darrin, out of fear he would be convinced that Mom was right. Sharing it with him was a turning point. Detached, he could see the manipulations for what it was and helped me put it aside.

When the wedding day came, she played her part as mother-of-the-bride with gusto, and there was no mention of The Letter, or the sentiments she had conveyed in it. It was as if The Letter had never been written. When she arrived, she boasted about the beautiful decorations and sought compliments for her new handmade dress, made special for her only daughter's wedding. It was, by the way, an exact replica of the dress I wore at Erica's graduation a couple of years before.

Years later, I received some closure in regards to The Letter. Jack had just gotten engaged to his second wife, Helen, and he too received The Letter from Mom. It was completely out of character for my mother to do or say *anything* to upset him. Jack, therefore, was completely unequipped to deal with the shock he would receive upon reading her scathing words. The message was so upsetting to Jack and Helen that they drove two hours to my house just to tell me about it. Even as I write this, I remember my outburst of laughter when he walked into my sunroom with The Letter in hand. I did apologize for laughing, but I just couldn't help it. By my forties, I was getting exceedingly good at predicting my mother's behavior, and I would be lying if I said I wasn't expecting a postmarked time bomb to arrive on Jack's doorstep as a last-ditch effort to change his mind. Admittedly, it was also somewhat reassuring to know I wasn't the only victim of her instability.

Unfortunately for Mom, The Letter led Jack and Helen to decide against inviting her to the wedding. They both feared she would make a spectacle of herself and put a damper on their day.

Their wedding went off without a hitch, or Mom, on a beautiful summer day in the White Mountains of New Hampshire. I played the role of mother-of-the-groom, sitting in the front row with my husband and children. Elizabeth sang as Helen and her children walked down the aisle, and the only tears shed were tears of joy.

As anticipated, the aftermath of the wedding was less joyful. Although it was Jack who had failed to mention anything about the wedding date to Mom, she found a way to see it as my fault. She felt it should have fallen on me to convince Jack and Helen to invite her, and as I did no such thing, I committed one more failure for which she could despise and blame me. Jack was completely off the hook – I was the one at fault. She welcomed Helen and her family with open arms, at least to their face, and all were forgiven— except for me.

18

The Bully with a Knife

When most people hear the word *bully,* the image that may come to mind is physical schoolyard bullying. You know...bigger kids beating up on smaller kids. This is only one type of bullying; there are so many other aspects that play into the terms *bullying* and *harassment.* Bullying is repetitive, intentional and an imbalance of power (or perceived power). Gossip, intimidation, exclusion, abuse of power, aggressive pressure and name-calling are all part of a wide-angle view of what bullying and harassment means in our societal age. Typically, a bully is a predator—somebody who has high but unstable self-esteem. During periods of instability, the bully will behave in ways that will allow them to regain that sense of high self-esteem. One of the most common behaviors is to put others down, giving the bully the sensation of being in power. Bullying most often happens in private, when no one is around to witness the incident. Victims are strategically isolated by the bully, so that they are trapped in a net only visible to the bully and their target. This way, if the aggressor is caught, they can easily shift blame and deny the allegations. Confident by nature, bullies are sneaky and cunning, experts at telling what looks like the truth—when in fact, they have just deceived everyone. The victim will typically respond in one of two ways, neither of which being ideal. Some stay silent out of fear, while others respond emotionally, making them appear unstable. When a victim is silent too long, or when a bully is left unchecked, the ramifications can be grave and long lasting-fear, anxiety, lashing out, emotional outbursts and even suicide.

I have spent twenty-two years teaching, studying, and advocating for laws and programs that protect our young people from the age-old culture of bullying, harassment and violence. I have always believed that bullying is a symptom of a much larger disease, which is a lack of good character, boundaries, respect, and the product of learned antisocial disorders that are taught to our children within their families. I am particularly drawn to parental and bystander training; teaching individuals about warning signs and how to recognize certain behaviors as unacceptable, and when to report so that they can be better equipped to assist children that suffer in silence.

When I started working to combat a shift in this culture, I began to recognize that it was my own life I was advocating for. I had no problem standing up for someone else if they experienced bullying, especially for my children, but I was incapable of doing the same for myself. On occasion, I have been labeled as too eager to jump up on my soapbox and stand up for others—a rebel. However, if I must add a label to my box, it would be activist. The disapproving looks I received would only spur me forward, determined to make a change to the world around me. Agatha Christie said it best; *A mother's love for her child is like nothing else in the world. It knows no law, no pity, it dares all things and crushes down remorselessly all that stands in its path.* This is who I am; it describes my reaction when I see anyone—family member or total stranger—become vulnerable to mistreatment. I had struggled my entire life sorting through the atypical lessons Mom taught me, knowing they were in opposition to what I innately knew to be right and wrong. I have imagined what it would have been like to have a trusted adult support me. Although I had never been taught proper social behaviors, my instincts were pure, and dead on–to love fiercely, and protect those I loved. Mom never had the emotional depth to ever reach this level of maturity. Her instincts never led her to nurturing behavior, she was too focused on her own personal gains, leaving me on the sidelines.

As I became an expert on bullying prevention, I realized that my passion for protecting children and combating domestic violence and abuse stemmed from my own history. It seems I spent many days trying to make up for something I failed to recognize long ago. I was robbed of my childhood, and by standing up for children who were suffering the same pain I experienced, in some way I was working to emend the sins of my mother.

It took years for me to apply the label "bully" to the matriarch of our home. Having been so tangled up in that cycle of emotional abuse, I had to step away from the family to finally gain perspective. My mother was the school-yard bully I could never quite escape. It was clear she was conducting her behavior out of sight for only me to see. My years of advocating for children helped me to recognize the toxic environment she created, but that very recognition helped me process my own trauma and thereby learn to also advocate for myself.

My mother's behavior was never clearer to me than at my granddaughter Alexandria's first birthday party. We all headed north to convene for a celebratory picnic in honor of Erica's baby girl. The party couldn't have been more perfect—a picturesque backyard setting for a celebration of this beautiful little life. Mom had placed herself beside Alexandria's high chair where all the attention was being directed. She was seemingly contentedly playing with the baby and sharing in the adoration. There were gifts, balloons, and a homemade Elmo birthday cake decorated with candles. When too much attention was placed on the baby and not Mom, she knew it was time to take control of the party and have all eyes on her. After going through a period of grooming, in this case, Alexandria and her parents, she moved on to use shock, awe, and guilt to maintain control. The shock and awe came from the over-the-top, emotionally charged statement unrelated to any of the existing conversations, Mom turned to the party at large and announced, "She looks more like an alien than a real baby, what is wrong with her?"

Shocked by this abhorrent comment, we were speechless; yet no one said anything, out of respect for the occasion. My daughter Erica, however, had reached her limit. Most normal people would. She found this dramatic reaction exhausting and strange.

She bit her tongue, knowing that confrontation would only worsen the situation. There was no point, as she recognized that this moment marked the end of a profoundly unfulfilling relationship for her. Years before I cut ties with Mom; Erica was adamant that her daughter would never be at the mercy of Mom's vile tongue as she had been.

Erica was not on Mom's favorites list and their relationship had always been strained, even at the best of times. Nevertheless, this comment put an end to any kind of association between the two, and Erica never spoke to her grandmother again. Though Mom never shied away from sharing these types of comments privately, no one was used to her voicing her thoughts so publicly. Usually these sentiments were communicated in a private conversation that would start out with, "I have a serious question for you". She would then give me a laundry list of what I should change with my daughters or say, "Why is that child so ugly"? Or, "Why is that person so fat"? "You should tell them to lose some weight". "Too bad your kids don't look like our family". The seriousness with which she would ask these questions was beyond my comprehension; I could never understand the value she placed on other people's physical appearance and her motivation for me to tell them to change. It was conceit to an extreme.

Once, Mom called me for a heart-to-heart, wanting to explain why she favored certain family members over others. Her favoritism was no surprise to me, but the brazen way she attempted to explain her reasoning was beyond overwhelming. She grimly looked at me with a seriousness in her voice and said, "I love your brother more because he was the firstborn son." This wasn't surprising, as Mom always favored Jack, and the fact that he was the first-born son was certainly the icing on the cake. She went on, "I love Elizabeth because she is my first grandchild, but Liam is adopted from Mexico, and so he *has* to be my favorite. That's just the way it is." She rationalized why Erica, Quinn and I were second best and needed to spell this out to put us in her rightful family hierarchy. Value for Mom was often measured by her own moments of self-importance or opportunities for future gain. To the average person, this rating system would not make sense. First, choosing favorites is not something a grandmother or parent usually does or admits to. Second, if the ethics are removed and logic is applied, it seems a pattern of first-borns would prevail, but that wasn't the case either. See, a firstborn is a memorable moment, one that involves celebratory bragging in the grocery store, wallet-sized photos of a rosy-cheeked baby to show off, but most important to her, it provided gushing attention, oohs and ahhs from friends and neighbors, a praising of the new proud grandmother. For Mom, those moments were great, but even greater was the humanitarian recognition, the added element of being able to say, "This is my grandson, my daughter adopted him from Mexico". Well, that, and the fact that he was a boy. Being a favorite for Mom wasn't always a prestigious position. Mom adored the attention she received when talking about the adoption of Liam, yet liked the perception of power even more. Mom believed she was better than Liam because of his nationality. In her mind, this gave her an ongoing upper hand. Quinn was the biological child of the evil son-in-law that wouldn't call her Nana; he didn't have a chance.

Fortunately, both of my sons couldn't care less about her whacky classification system – their interaction with her was limited by their young age and distance. It did, however, create significant tension between my mother and my daughters, as well as between my brother and I.

Her heart-to-hearts were outrageous. I remember another, when she asked me, "How do you handle the voices in your head." I didn't understand.

"What are you talking about?" I remarked.

"You know, when you are lying in bed thinking and you have all these voices telling you what to do—racing and jarring thoughts. Do you have that?"

"No I don't. What are they saying to you?" But when I questioned her and she noticed my confusion, the conversation swiftly changed. I often wondered if she really did experience voices or was she toying with me, it was never really clear.

Although interactions with Mom were few and far between, we learned to expect an incident each time there was a visit. I tried to keep our socializing confined to one of our private homes, to limit the opportunity for her to create a public spectacle—but this was somewhat inevitable.

One instance played out when I took Mom and a friend to see Elizabeth play piano in a local theater production of *Jesus Christ Superstar*.

Leaving the husbands at home to care for the kids, my friend Margaret, Mom, and I set out for the long-anticipated girls' night out. Stopping at a local grocery store to purchase some candy and drinks for the show, Mom discovered she didn't have any money to pay for her snacks. Rummaging through her purse, she instead pulled out a Bowie hunting knife in a handsome leather case. Her hand wrapped tightly around the hilt, she laid the knife on the counter with the sharp tip pointed directly at the cashier.

The cashier slowly retreated from striking range. A look of shock flashed across his face. I swiftly jumped forward and grabbed her hand, saying quickly, "She is just kidding, she carries that for protection." I thrust some money at the clerk, and ushered my mother out the door, followed closely by a stunned Margaret.

I asked her why she would do such a thing. She responded oddly in laughter with some self-satisfied smugness and said "Oh, he can't take a joke!" And that was it; she set up the scene for being the center of attention and without remorse, it was over.

We managed to keep her under control for the rest of the evening, although I can't say that I enjoyed myself. I was humiliated by her behavior, and mortified that Margaret had to witness her "joke". At the end of the night, I was so relieved to have left the show without my mother causing any embarrassment for Elizabeth, as she had done for me.

My daughters are incredibly talented, motivated, and successful in their own right—both fantastic mothers, and strong, opinionated women. More importantly, they are loving, compassionate, and kind in their personal and professional lives. In spite of having a teen mom with no experience or life skills, they have grown to be astonishing people. They handled their grandmother in their own unique way, and I can only applaud them for how they managed their relationships with her. Much better than I did.

19

A True Gentleman

Relationships are like puzzles, made up of colorful and strangely-shaped pieces, and after a certain amount of time these vignettes all mesh together to paint a picture of the connection between two individuals. It could take a day, it could take weeks— but once finished, it helps to create an understanding of the relationship.

The puzzle I shared with my mother was one of contradictory messages and misshapen pieces that didn't fit together. Pieces that could change shape at a frustrating velocity, and without warning. With the help of many years of soul searching, I have been able to decipher these stories and place them into a shape that began to make sense within the puzzle. To begin the decoding process, I found it only fitting to tell my mother's version of my birth story.

For as long as I can remember, Mom would tell the agonizing story of childbirth and the part I played in the destruction of her body. “YOU had the biggest head of any baby ever born. In fact, the doctor said YOU had the biggest head he had ever seen”. “YOU ripped me from belly button to asshole”. This was Mom's grandiose birth story, told to me and any other women who ever tried sharing their labor and delivery stories with her.

Mom claimed that she had the longest labor, the largest episiotomy, and most gigantic-headed baby ever born, regardless of the fact that she also claimed to have delivered three and a half months prematurely. She was insistent in her need to feel unique, special, and too good for the average story. She routinely fabricated close relationships with prominent people, stories about places she had never been, and events she hadn't attended. Unfortunately, though she believed herself to be an accomplished socialite, she fell grossly short when it came to the knowledge of socially-accepted norms, behaviors, words, phrases, or terminology. Her crème de la crème self-image was crushed by her lack of social grace, civic involvement and vulgar vocabulary. I found myself sometimes feeling sorry for her, as I watched her flounder while attempting to one-up others, or argue a case that she knew nothing about – embarrassing herself in the process. She also didn't do well corroborating and fact checking with herself on her own fictitious stories. The birth story proved to be one that was just too much for her to manage; she was drowning in lies and creating new ones to cover up additions to her stories. One day she finally got so deep in her inconsistencies, she casually added, "If I had delivered Debbie full-term, she would have been over twelve pounds."

This was more than just her arrogance or vanity. Her inherent need to invent a dramatized version of reality, that was always superior and outrageously exaggerated, had to be due to something more than ego. Therefore, I began removing some of the puzzle pieces that didn't fit. I already had my first hint at the infamous 25th wedding anniversary party, and it was clear that she had been pregnant when they got married. No big deal, but why she kept bringing up the story of my birth was something I couldn't fully understand.

The story of my birth is an example of how she would attempt to rewrite history by taking a normal part of our lives and influencing it to do her bidding. Some was true, some was not, some was clear and some simply unbelievably disgraceful. It left people shaking their heads in uncertainty. If my mother said the sky was green, then it was simply green. You didn't argue, and it would have been worthless to try. To say I learned to "pick my battles" would be a drastic understatement.

After I suffered two miscarriages, she then said she had two miscarriages between Jack and I. The magnitude of her exaggerations even extended to her redrafting her obituary, that I originally wrote with her. In it, she wrote that she went to college at one of the schools I attended. Her version that she rewrote, listed a college that wasn't even in existence when she was of college age. Subtle, believable but not true.

To be honest, we would agree with anything she said if it meant avoiding her wrath. Mom was particularly sensitive and quick to react to even the smallest criticisms or challenges. She perceived any corrections (like the sky is blue, not green) as an unfathomable personal attack. Dad chose his battles strategically, usually by refraining from any type of participation whatsoever. He learned to ignore Mom and let the small things go – and sadly, that included me.

I am inclined to believe that my dad began questioning my mother about the specifics behind my paternity soon after I was born. I refuse to believe he didn't, at some point, question the story of my wildly premature arrival, being the smart man he was. It also wouldn't surprise me if he ignored the issue entirely and stayed tightly wrapped in her web. We will never know.

On two separate occasions as an adult, Dad took me aside to tell me what a "true gentleman" was. Same story, two times. "A gentleman will not touch a woman until he marries her. This is out of respect. I didn't touch your mother until our wedding night," he stated firmly. It was just like the time Aunt Bert told me about the 25th anniversary, with a tone of secrecy.

At that moment, I giggled to myself, and found it to be very odd; why would he deem it important to tell me that? But I was missing the point, the proof was in the pudding, but I didn't bite. I thought he was referring to my first husband, implying that he didn't find him to be a gentleman. I felt this to be irrelevant, as this kind of cautionary advice was simply too little, too late. I didn't understand that he was trying to prepare me for what he knew to be coming – the realization that he wasn't my biological father.

20

A Trip to the Wonderful Land of Oz

Author L. Frank Baum has to be one of the greatest children's fantasy writers of all time. The imagination he used to create *The Wonderful Land of Oz* was groundbreaking in American literature. I have often compared our family dynamic to this classic story. Mom as the antagonist to my protagonist. I was Dorothy with Toto in tow, and she was the Wicked Witch of the West.

At the start of the story, the Witch was in control of Dorothy; manipulating, intimidating, taking her dog away, and creating fear whenever she chose—which forced Dorothy to live in a constant state of alarm and created a chronic need to plot an escape. Although it seemed to Dorothy an impossible task to rid herself of the Wicked Witch, in the end, the solution lay simply in a pail of water. It took bravery and determination for Dorothy to use the power of the water to melt the witch and save herself from the abuse, as all other avenues failed her. Similarly, it took me many years to discover, process, and save myself from my mother's hidden abuse.

As an adult, I had tried for many years to reason with Mom, asking her to respect my boundaries. I realized she was never going to change; she loved who she was, knew what she was doing and fed off her perceived power over me. I was well-practiced in enduring the maltreatment she aimed at me. However, once I saw it being aimed at my children and grandchildren, I felt myself snap. I tolerated her maltreatment of me, I was used to it, but I would never allow her to harm my children. Therefore, I used my pail of water – I cut all ties.

It took several years of therapy and self-analysis to help me accept that using my proverbial water pail was okay, and I didn't owe her any more chances at redemption. Therapy was more than just revisiting past memories; it was the first step on the road to recovery. Being a child that was maltreated, I came to understand my subconscious triggers, and how the abuse began. I desperately wanted to jump in the water and swim away but realized I first needed to learn how to swim or else I would drown. I did this by testing the water—first by moving away, then by distancing myself, and eventually by cutting all ties. It was a colossal life changing moment when I realized I was living in fear, always waiting for the *alarm to go off* at any given moment. This impacted my ability to mentally focus and plan ahead, as it was all I could handle simply being in the moment, partly due to the heavy exhaustion I carried with me everywhere. The energy I burned trying to interpret and identify her nonverbal cues was unfathomable. I never had the chance to do the things most children had the opportunity to do, like playing with friends, clubs, dancing lessons, deciding on what clothes to wear, even enjoying school. I had spent my life not thinking about months from now or any type of future; I was hyper focused only on my current threat. Nothing lay beyond my prison cell.

As an infant I was bathed, fed, and held by this woman. I automatically trusted her. This created the love-bombing stage, when she loved and showered me with my basic needs, only to destructively manipulate me as soon as I was old enough to do her bidding. This is why I always thought the problem was me. I had nothing to compare my experience to, not the way adults do. The effects on a child are different than an adult dealing with a toxic relationship because it is all they have ever known. This left me in need of trauma recovery therapy and of reparenting myself in adulthood. It took a long time to realize there was something wrong. Thinking back, there were never good times, just times that weren't so bad. When times seemed good, I was on alert, perched on a time bomb waiting for it to explode, and unable to enjoy the moment.

I experienced all the classic feelings of not being heard or acknowledged, being the parent not the child, low self-esteem, being afraid to be myself, trust and abandonment issues, the keeper of secrets, and emotional emptiness. My childhood development was stunted and robbed. I was judged by my physical appearance and had no idea what a healthy role model was.

Therapy provided a profound clarity in these areas along with some others as well, which included my need for instant gratification. Not knowing when something good would come along, I grabbed it and held on for dear life, taking as much as I could: food, love, attention. As time went on, I developed certain habits when reacting to nonverbal cues that caused puzzling sensitivities other people would normally brush off—gentle teasing that was mistaken as psychologically degrading, or a friendly touch that reminded me of my sickening grandfather. My mother's parenting style conditioned me to be fearful and caused an adult-onset anxiety disorder by the time I was twenty-four.

Consequently, I perceived the world as a war zone and I was always on the front line. It wasn't until I was in my thirties that I began to rethink the belief system that caused my fears and feelings of emptiness. It's understandable: Mom's reach was great and she took the liberty to invade boundaries. I was sensitive, and guilt-ridden which made me want to please her all the time. The gratification of accommodating her every wish made me the detective in the relationship. Fixing everything was an attempt to gain her love and serve.

I remember one day when Mom called me while I was working. It was one of the last times I would speak to her. Several years before, she decided it would be a good idea to put her house in her children's names and plan for her future. The plan being if she needed help or money, Jack and I could sell her house and pay for long term care expenses. The house, which was paid in full, was given to my brother and I to manage equally. Jack was the one to make physical repairs and I oversaw all medical, financial, and legal issues. This worked well for several years until Mom decided she wanted the house back. This knee jerk reaction was triggered when Jack called her one day to confide in her about some disagreement in his marriage.

Heaven knows what was said in the conversation, but Mom's solution was to have me sign the house over to Jack so he would have a place to live in the event that his wife left him, or he lost his job or whatever else may come. Jack, at the time, was married with three grown stepchildren. He had a very good position with a leading supply chain management company for thirty plus years and was fifty-four.

I explained to her that I wasn't going to hand over the house for such a silly reason without discussing it. I tried to explain that Jack was venting, probably not asking for help, and the house was her long-term care security. Most of all, Jack was financially stable enough with a hefty retirement plan to take care of himself if hard times fell on him.

During the conversation, I noticed a click on the phone and a change in her personality. She had me on speaker because an attorney was at her house listening to our conversation.

"Do you think you want to move back to Dexter and live in this house?" Mom asked.

“No,” I replied. “I have no plan or desire to move. Why are you asking?”

“I want you to give the house to your brother so he can live here when his wife kicks him out,” she said in a matter-of -fact tone.

“What makes you think that is going to happen?” I asked.

“He called. He's upset, I need to help him.”

Distracted by the clicking sound on the phone, I asked, “Is someone listening in on our conversation?”

I heard a muffled voice say, “Here,” as she passed the phone over to the person listening in. Without explanation or warning, I found myself in a conversation with an unknown person. Honestly, I thought it was one of Mom's friends and he sounded a bit intoxicated, which had happened before. I couldn't understand a word he was saying. He was mumbling and speaking very fast. I asked who he was and he gave me his name. “Attorney Craig Ryan,” he bluntly stated. “Your mother wants her house back.” I hung up. I sent my brother a message and asked him what caused Mom to hire an attorney to get the house back in her name. I explained that every time he tells her his problems she wants me to “fix them” for him. Jack didn't respond to my message and didn't call me again until he was ready to sell the house after her death, which was six years later.

After trying to reach Jack and his wife, I looked up the attorney's name and called his office. Explaining the situation in brief to his secretary I asked to speak to Mr. Ryan, expecting clarification that he was indeed not at my mother's house that day. She put me through. Shockingly, it was him that I spoke with when my mother called. He was Australian, had a very heavy accent and spoke abnormally fast.

I was very clear that his tactics of calling me and not identifying that he was listening in on a private call, was immoral and sleazy. Mr. Ryan responded, "Well your mother wanted me to do it. She wanted to show me that you didn't want to live here and thought maybe I could convince you to sign the house over to your brother. She wants him to have it to live in." Even this educated man couldn't reason with Mom. It intrigued me how one could manipulate someone so easily. I wasn't surprised, only hurt and reminded of the several other times this had happened in the past.

One time in particular comes to mind. When I was eighteen and a mother of two toddlers, Dad informed me he was getting ready to cash in an insurance policy he had purchased to pay for my college or future. I was not planning on attending college any time soon, but Dad thought the money would be helpful to my new little family because of the many things we needed–a washing machine, hot water and a bathroom, to name a few. A couple of months later, I asked when the money would be available, and was told by my parents, "It came in a while back and we used it to buy Jack the snowmobile he wanted so desperately."

This was always the case; whether it was one cookie left in the jar or an insurance payout, the choice was made in favor of Jack.

This story weighed on me as I called Mom after the conversation with Mr. Ryan. I tried to reason with her about the house but to no avail. That was the breakaway point for me. Everything I had worked toward fell into place. The pail of water was at my feet and I was ready. I was in the midst of therapy and was trying to come to terms with the abuse and whether I should cut all ties or not. She made the decision easier and in that moment I used the pail of water to melt the ties of that dysfunctional relationship. I had given her more chances than she deserved. I begged her to stop, only to watch her up the ante, trying all that much harder to infiltrate my boundaries and test my limits. She continually crafted stories and orchestrated theatrical performances that would put any Broadway show to shame, driven by what seemed to be an infinite reserve of energy. It was then that I realized her energy source was me. I was her fuel. She spent years draining my tank, racking up a bill and never making a deposit. It was time to shut off the power. Her gaslighting days would end here. It would be the last time I would speak to her, or so I thought.

A couple weeks later, while on a ladder painting my bedroom, the landline phone rang in my office. Being a work day, I jumped off the ladder and ran to pick it up without viewing the number on the caller ID.

"Hello?" I waited but there was no response and looked down at the number. It was Mom. She eventually spoke, but her words weren't logical.

"Why are you calling?" She asked.

"What?" I was confused. *What the hell was she talking about*, I thought. *She* called me. One would think I would have caught on to her dangling bait after all these years, she nibbled on the *what*, but then gained momentum.

"I was just sitting here drinking my tea at the kitchen table and the phone rang. I looked down and your number was on the screen, so I answered it," she claimed in her gaslighting way.

"What" was the last thing I ever said to her. I felt an overwhelming feeling of clarity. I hung up and the relationship was terminated just like that, I had made the decision to sink or swim.

For the first few years, Mom relentlessly tried to make contact, either through sending The Letter, or via third parties such as her lawyer or Aunt Bert. What had initially been so hard to escape from, was suddenly very easy to let go. Her attempts of triangulation proved fruitless, as I was simply done. Her power over me was gone and she no longer had any control.

I finally gave myself permission to let go of the dysfunctional relationship which no longer served me. Once I said goodbye, the estrangement I experienced mirrored the process of death after a long illness—grief ensued just the same. I knew it was coming but wasn't sure exactly when, or how I would feel when it did arrive. It was inevitable, yet I mourned the death of our relationship just the same, even though it had never, and would never, become the bond I needed from a mother figure. Hope was gone, replaced by reality. We would never have mother-daughter talks, there would be no fond memories made over shopping trips or cooking together, we would not spend time making plans for the holidays, and I would not have that trusted confidant to call when I needed a shoulder to cry on. Our story ended with me carrying the maternal role, never having had a real mother of my own—I would never experience the role of the child.

This realization was my cross to bear but ended up having everlasting benefits. I thought that in breaking my bond with her, I would be distancing myself from my childhood, my hometown, my family and friends. I came to terms to relinquish my claim on them all. However, this would not be the case—I was yet again in for quite a surprise.

Just like the story of *The Wizard of Oz,* the death of the antagonist enables all the flying monkeys and all the dutiful soldiers to come forward, express gratitude and confess their true feelings—opinions they had held close the whole time.

Following the estrangement, I was inundated with relatives, friends, and acquaintances sharing their own stories of the chaos and upheaval they had been subjected to by her. I was not alone in suffering at her machinations. I had severed the relationship on my own, but death had severed the relationship between Mom, her remaining family and friends. As the news of our estrangement trickled out, the sympathizers engulfed me in waves. Some fast and furious, some warm and comforting, and still others more trivial. Some of the stories I heard left me dumbfounded. Revelations that had finally come to me in my adulthood had been obvious to so many people, for so long – I was simply late to the party. As their stories came to light, I couldn't help but wonder why none of these individuals came forward earlier—how could they have allowed so many years to go by without wondering about my happiness and well-being as a child? Then it became clear: many of them had deliberately avoided me, as they assumed I was just like my mother, and others didn't know the intensity of the problem. Avoidance was accomplished simply through silence.

My relatives started contacting me once they knew Mom and I were no longer speaking, and suddenly I had a family that was welcoming me back, arms wide open.

There were even friends from Jack's past calling to test the waters—among them his ex-wife and his best friend. Hours of conversations and stories flew from both sides, comparing our respective encounters with the Marilyn Madness.

After she passed away, there was a second wave. A flood of people contacted me with condolences, which very quickly turned into personal horror stories. I listened, not because I felt responsible, but because it validated so much of my history. I prepared myself for the unburdening of everyone she had ever come in contact with. I thought I was alone, but her victims appeared in droves—particularly teens, now adults, that used to hang out at her house, the elderly, and the lonely. It made sense. She sought out the vulnerable. Each individual responded to Mom's antics in a variety of ways; some took it on the chin, while others figured it out and chose to avoid her. One person confessed that he would leave a store if he even saw her. Another woman, so embarrassed, shared her story and asked that it never be told.

She knew how to pick her victims, and she knew how to keep them separate as well; compartmentalizing was her sixth sense. She would listen carefully while calculating, spinning stories and plotting her triangulation. Her tactics ranged from using their own secrets to control them, to complaining how people were taking advantage of her, financially or emotionally, in order to elicit sympathy from those she deemed to be an ideal victim. She would isolate, manipulate, and confuse even the most astute of prey. By the time we buried her ashes a year after her passing, the stories had come from life-long friends, neighbors, relatives, employees at the local grocer, and even the workers at the cemetery – no soul had escaped an encounter in Marilyn's web.

21

Labels

Working through each part of my life with a therapist took a lot of time. This process was something I could discover only through detailed retrospective analysis.

My childhood psychological toy box was overflowing with labels, echoing my mother's voice. *What is wrong with you? You are a hairy monkey, big head, clown feet, fat, lazy, ugly, never amount to anything, unlovable, ruined my life, you need to fix it and it is all your fault.* Each word was a bullet to my wounded heart. When I traded in my dysfunctional toy box for a tool box that would better serve my needs, I wasn't aware of how deeply wounded I was, and that I would continue to struggle with these insecurities after they had lain dormant for so many years. Therapy and time helped sort them out and rid me of what I didn't need anymore, leaving behind only the tools I deemed helpful to my emotional health.

I had always thought of my mother to be crazy—not from a scientific standpoint, but as part of her odd personality. I've stopped using that word because I now know she deserves a legitimate label in my box. I can only explain her illness based on my experiences as a target of narcissistic victim syndrome. Although Mom demonstrated a cluster of signs and symptoms of personality disorders such as narcissism, sociopathy, psychopathy, it is impossible to pinpoint an exact disorder without a proper diagnosis. Depending on the situation or day, Mom could swing back and forth, leading to the conclusion that she was a narcopath, a pop-psychology term for a person who shows all the signs of meeting the diagnostic criteria for at least two personality disorder classifications. This term is consistent with her gaslighting, triangulation, manipulation and subterfuge used to influence and control others. The disturbing part is she could calculate a plot, follow it through and laugh in my face while watching you go under. This is very hard to understand, and experts can't answer why a narcissist does such mean things, other than they feel emotionally deprived. As the target searches to escape into a place of comfort, the narcissist craves their energy of compassion and empathy that they are resistant to. When the target does well in any aspect of life, the narcissist views it as they are doing something wrong, which then creates retaliation. It is a cat and mouse game at its finest. The cat taunts the mouse before they devour them and no one is the wiser, seeing it as a normal way of life.

Mom would be on a high any time she was in range of people she could glean attention from. Attention was like a drug for her and if it wasn't available, she would create it. It took so much energy to be the star of the show that she was prone to crash for days at a time, and the lows were just as alarming as the highs. When she was down, Dad would say, "Your mother works so hard and is worn out, she needs to rest. Let's just let her rest." "Worn out" was a common phrase in our family. Although some of these traits mirror bipolar disorder, anxiety and depression, to my knowledge she was never officially diagnosed.

As a child, survival meant being the servant and peace keeper in our home. I served Mom like the queen she believed herself to be; training to be one of her flying monkeys. She expected me to pay constant attention and show boundless admiration to her, without any consideration for my own needs. If she had a grievance, it was my obligation to be the sympathetic listener and if she had a problem, I was the one that needed to take responsibility and fix it. She spent so many years trying to make me believe that she was superior, better than all others, and that she was entitled to anything she wanted. All the while, instilling in me an inferiority complex that would take years to shake off.

Trying to rearrange my past to uncover something that made sense, I struggled with the dissonance between how I was treated and how I appeared to be treated. I had a sturdy roof over my head in a middle-class home. What did I have to complain about? Everything on the outside looked normal, but everything on the inside was a jumbled mess. That's what psychological abuse looks like—normal on the outside, utter chaos on the inside.

When I was young, I didn't know my mother was any different than anyone else. I thought all mothers acted like her, and I had very little context to understand the unconventionality of her behavior and assumed that what went on in my house was also occurring in all homes. Again, I thought I was the problem. It was, after all, what I had always been told. This being the norm, I never thought to talk about it.

Not too long ago I was talking with a few cousins about their experiences with my mother. They asked me, "When did you know your mother was crazy?"

I replied, "I guess when I was in my forties. When did you know?"

Looking at me with puzzling grins, they both replied, "We have always known."

I have read every book, blog, article and website I could get my hands on, trying to gain some clarity in regards to my family dynamics. Was it discord and confusion, all a figment of my imagination? Or was it deliberately created by my mother? Then I came across the book, *You're Not Crazy - It's Your Mother: Understanding and Healing for Daughters of Narcissistic Mothers,* by Danu Morrigan. Just reading the title made me burst into laughter and tears at the same time, and I read every word of the book as if my life depended on it. It felt like the book was written for and about me; a book describing experiences I had and symptoms my mother displayed—it whispered to me from the shelf, *buy me, buy me.* As soon as the book was in my hands I didn't set it down until I was finished, hanging on every word. This discovery spurred me to order several more books about mother-daughter relationships that focused on narcissism, antisocial personality disorders, child and psychological abuse, and I read them all within a few weeks.

Around the same time, Darrin and I had traveled to New Orleans for a long weekend. While he attended a conference, I spent the entire trip absorbed in the pages of these books and only left our French Quarter townhouse to eat. It was like someone was reading my mind, recounting my whole life, writing it down and helping me make sense of it page by page. One of the books focused specifically on the tactic of gaslighting (the term to manipulate someone by psychological means into questioning their own sanity) and ironically, I could look right out the window and down Bourbon Street to a hotel that would light gas lanterns each night outside their lobby.

Fate was showing me the light, quite literally. My experience with antisocial personality disorders was limited, or so I thought. Boy, was I wrong. I had lived it, it was as common as eating and sleeping. It didn't mimic the portrayal seen in movies; it was much more subtle, a secret between my mother and I. The abuse was hidden and trivial in comparison to most child abuse cases people read about, the ones where people hang on every word in disbelief. This type of hidden behavior is often overlooked or not seen by the naked eye. The constant belittling, shaming, humiliating, name calling or making negative comparisons was served up daily with threats of abandonment, bullying and rejection on the side. Paired with limited hugs, kisses, or other signs of affection, it was brutal on my emotional development.

My mother had a personality disorder, but was she narcissistic, or mentally ill? My mind was racing with questions. It did make a difference—I needed to know if she treated me this way because she had a disease, or whether it was intentional. And if she was mentally ill, why didn't she get help or why didn't others call her on her behavior? Why didn't her mother, her father, sisters or her husband ever seek help for her?

Perhaps they did, and she refused. I went through every checklist I could find in my books, and everything they described had been apparent in my mother and in my home. I started reading about children whose parents make them into narcissists. I remember thinking to myself, *Nana couldn't have done such a thing as that...not intentionally. Not the loving, sweet woman that gave me all the love I remember from my childhood.*

Even though my mission was to get some closure for my own sake, I found myself still grasping for a diagnosis I could attach to my mother. I started unpacking her childhood, attempting to identify reasons for her insidious behavior. I read that narcissism was learned behavior, not a disease, which fit with her upbringing; the coddled, prized youngest child, a survivor in the wake of a younger sibling's death coupled by a father that ruled with an iron fist. But this was speculation—I lacked the proper qualifications and knowledge to diagnose, and I was getting off track. In fact, I incessantly ask myself the question *"Why?"* and had been since I was seven. Although it doesn't nearly get the credit it deserves in our society, I recognized I was now using the question *"Why?"* as a crutch to postpone my healing. This was how I prevented myself from facing the reality of major hints from the past. In this case, trying to figure out what was wrong with my mother instead of focusing on healing myself. My task was to unpack my own issues and process them in a healthy way.

When I read that people with personality disorders are extremely resistant to changing their behavior, it was like the lights had come on and I could finally see. Examining Mom's behavior helped me see that she had some sort of disorder, and being the dutiful daughter I was, my job was to fix it for her. I was now retreating and trying to take care of her again. I called her doctors. It didn't help. She did humor me and went to the appointments I arranged only to convince them nothing was wrong with her; it was her interfering daughter and she would handle it.

Getting back on track, I came to the realization that people with parallel behaviors as Mom were drawn to me. Similarly, I was attracted to them, as their behavior was familiar, even if it was unhealthy. So many times in my life I allowed people to capture me in their ghastly web of egotistical power plays, manipulations, and silent abuse. It was imperative for me to begin setting some boundaries and sever connections if needed, to ensure this would no longer happen.

As expected, the separation from my mother was the hardest bond to break, however, once I was aware and understood the warning signs more clearly, my boundaries became stronger and I was able to recognize other dysfunctional relationships in my life. I was learning to not be an easy target and learning what I needed to move on emotionally.

22

Time Discovers Truths

When I was about to send my last child off to college, I thought that therapy would be helpful. I had been a mom for over forty years, and every day for these forty years I made dinner, drove my children to music lessons or a soccer game, balancing my job, life as mom, wife, business owner, and everything else. For several of those years I was a single mom, working full time. Working sixty hours a week as an administrator, I would take my lunch breaks late in the afternoon and drive to field hockey or soccer games and return to work to finish up the day after the games were over, or bring work home on nights and weekends.

With the last child leaving the house, I didn't know what I was going to do with my extra time. There was going to definitely be a huge void; a void I didn't want to face or even think about. My kids were gone and now it was just Darrin and I. What to do with that time? Well it was simple, and I recommend it to everyone who sends their last child to college: take a trip to Europe for three weeks. When we returned, we got a cat, and the adjustment wasn't as dramatic as I thought it was going to be. My fear of change had hindered the excitement of a new beginning and transformation in my life.

I made an appointment with a therapist two years before Liam and Quinn graduated high school. I was transparent with this new counselor about my intentions and goals, and then we began to explore why I was really there. He played along at first. It wasn't about the kids leaving, it was about my past and upbringing. In the first ten minutes, I explained my concerns about starting my life without children in my home and I don't think we ever talked about it again.

Sessions quickly turned to who I was and who I am, what I was searching for, and issues I had been subconsciously suppressing all my life.

I loved the sessions with my therapist, Adam. I could feel the growth week by week, year by year. I had worked with a therapist on many occasions; when I had my miscarriages, career planning, and when I supervised an MSW program while I was working at a university. I was a fan of the familiarity of the counseling process and appreciated its outcomes.

What I thought would be a few sessions turned into five years of coining my own phrase, "What Would Adam Say?" I used it frequently when contemplating a life decision I was struggling with. For some time, I had approached life like I was strategically building a puzzle. I busied myself by moving pieces around and trying to make them fit in the wrong places. When they didn't, I walked away and returned later. Sometimes I deliberately passed over the pieces that would fit, but didn't want to pick them up, or even really acknowledge them.

During those few years of weekly sessions, I became serious about addressing a lifetime of ignoring my gut feelings. I continued to study and research narcissism, ad nauseam.

I began to uncover a complete set of encyclopedias on the narration of my life, from birth to adulthood. It was mesmerizing, intoxicating, and in many ways comforting; what I was feeling was real. Even as I write these words I can feel the pain and stress draining from my body, freeing up space for growth and solace.

I realized that I had been raised in a toxic situation and had to make a clean break or I would never heal. I needed years of therapy to get me to that point. The process supplied me with the parenting I never had. It was clear that without therapy I would not succeed. It helped me through my understanding of what was missing from my formative years. I was learning about why I made certain choices, that it was okay to read countless books, have feelings, put myself first, search for answers to repair the damage that the psychological abuse inflicted, and gain some clarity and justification. What I had experienced was real; it had happened to other people who did survive and I would as well.

I asked Adam what diagnosis he had attached to me, wondering what he put on the insurance forms to get reimbursed. There was no name for it as far as I was concerned.

When he said PTSD, (post-traumatic stress disorder), I was puzzled and sort of chuckled. That was a little extreme, I thought. That is a serious condition that veterans suffered from after coming home from a war. My Dad suffered from it. I was not anywhere near or deserving of a severe diagnosis like that, my life wasn't that bad. Was I leading my counselor down the wrong path? And there it was, laid out on the table for me to see: reality.

I had lived on an emotional rollercoaster, the ups and downs with no seat belt, permission or a way to exit, forced to sit on a ride that I didn't want to be on in the first place. I lived parallel lives, conscious and unconscious, suppressing memories that were too painful to accept and making excuses to myself that life just wasn't that bad.

Chronic psychological abuse and manipulation is just as devastating as physical and sexual abuse, although I had experienced both of these as well. I didn't deserve to be labeled with that diagnosis; I was unworthy, ashamed, and broken.

When I finally came to accept the diagnosis of PTSD, I knew there was no way out of it. If I didn't do something now, my childhood memories would haunt me forever and I would never be free to move in a positive direction. After a lifetime of Mom attaching labels to me, I finally had a label that not only was accurate, but was helpful.

One thing was definite: everything was now falling in place. I understood the pattern, found the strength and gained the tools to pull myself up or out of an unhealthy situation.

My mother's lack of parenting made me feel guilty, wrong, hideous, unloved, obligated, undeserving, vulnerable and insignificant. Becoming mindful that the role of a parent was to love unconditionally, nurture and teach respect, I started to extend myself some empathy.

My body and mind needed to be peaceful, calm and sane. Therapy taught me that no relationship, blood relative or not, was worth compromising my own mental and physical health. I was an expert at running from the past but I wouldn't find peace unless I took yet another leap into the fire. The breakup would have to happen, even if it meant everyone in the family would never speak to me again, not that there were many of them. It would be my mother, Jack, and possibly Aunt Bert, who always asked me not to tell her sister she was contacting me or *she would be in trouble*. My fear was that they would think I was an ungrateful daughter, mean to an old lady, and selfish. I decided it was none of my business what others thought of me. I couldn't do anything about it. I can only live as my best self.

This didn't happen overnight; it took a very long time of hard work to process these deep thoughts and feelings. Yet, even after all these years of therapy, I still struggle to balance the lifelong effects of flashbacks, being easily startled or experience PTSD episodes of anxiety and fear. Recognizing the reason why my PTSD occurs has helped tremendously. It only last for a few seconds and I have the proper tools to return to reality, reassure myself and understanding the cause of my feelings in that moment.

23

The Sins of the Mother

My fifth child was born in 1999, in the form of a nonprofit after-school organization, Crossroads Youth Center. This safe haven was meant to be Darrin's postgraduate project for our church, but over the course of twenty-one years it evolved from a statewide program, then extended to national and international levels. My dedication to Crossroads was (and still is) truly akin to a mother's love for her child, and I was completely absorbed in the development and mission of the program. It was like a window had blown open, allowing a flood of ideas, strategies, information, and potential opportunities to wash over me. After it's conception, it took no time at all for Darrin and I to realize that our small-scale project had the capability to expand internationally, and could grow to include at-risk youth, children in need of after-school activities, latchkey kids, and other teens wanting to volunteer and mentor others. What had begun as a college project was already growing into a full-fledged safety net for youth in need. Crossroads wasn't a simple project at all—it was a mission of love. We began it as a program that would provide a safe environment for young people to turn to when in need, and it soon grew into an educational outreach program that teaches communities, parents, and families about the importance of raising resilient children. We advocate for teaching young people about tolerance and acceptance, and most importantly, we hope to prepare children to make healthy decisions when faced with scenarios that potentially expose them to risks. I donned my super-girl cape, and vowed to change the part of the world that I could reach—my own community.

The transformation Crossroads underwent was remarkable, growing from five people on day one to thousands of people involved today. We address social awareness issues, character education, and community involvement in the lives of children. From domestic violence, to drug abuse and child abuse, we've tackled them all. I'm proud to say we've been able to change the lives of people within and outside our local community, by providing educational resources and creating connections in order for our youth to live safe lives.

In the beginning, I was amazed at the amount of issues surrounding latchkey kids, youth suicide, and the lack of state laws protecting school-age students from bullying, harassment, and discrimination. I was unexpectedly passionate about these issues and the subject quickly drew me in. I became compelled to dive deeper and deeper into causes. As time went on, the issues became familiar and personal. Although it may seem obvious, it took several years for me to discover that Crossroads was a do-over for me. I subconsciously created an entire non-profit organization in my spare time to make up for my mother's sins, after-school shenanigans and for my childhood difficulties. I believed myself to be on the breaking edge of something new, something revolutionary, only to eventually discover that with each new story, each new Crossroads member, I was only rewriting my past to create a different narrative of my childhood. I was working to make life better for someone else, so they did not have the same adverse experiences I did, and if they did, provide them with the tools and confidence to not only survive these experiences, but to overcome them. I finally had a voice, and I still advocate for children nonstop today. It is an immeasurably satisfying and comforting feeling to know we make a positive difference in the lives of so many.

24

Coined a Thief

A short time before I officially severed ties with Mom, we went to visit for the weekend. While the kids were playing outside, Mom pulled out a gray metal box, in which she kept old coins from the forties and other small items that she believed would someday be of value. She asked Darrin to help her research to see if the coins were worth anything more than face value, and he willingly obliged. Purchasing a coin book and scouring the internet for coin appraisals, he spent hours searching for something of value in her collection, to no avail.

All he discovered was a Kennedy half-dollar worth $20, a few pennies that were worth a few dollars each, and approximately $50 in coins at face value. All totaled, her collection was worth about $75. We presented her with all the evidence we had uncovered, assuring her that the collection had no real value. We had taken a few of these coins home with us to evaluate further and try to sell for her, but again found nothing of value. We packaged the coins up and later returned them to her via mail.

Despite being presented with hard evidence, she maintained that three of the dimes in her collection held tremendous value, and she kept them in a kiss-lock leather change purse that had belonged to her mother. The black coin purse sat perched on her computer stand for months, safe and constantly under watch—until one day, it was gone.

Months later, I received a very confusing phone call from Mom. Having just returned home from a day trip to Boston with friends, I was standing in the driveway waving goodbye when Darrin opened the door to tell me I had a phone call. I hurried into the house to answer the call. After I said "hello", all I heard was shrieking.

"Where are my dimes? I want my dimes!" My mother's voice came blasting through the phone, accompanied by hysterical crying and what sounded like doors being slammed in the background. Caught completely off-guard, I tried (and failed) to calm her down and was eventually forced to hang up the phone, for lack of a better solution. Knowing there was no use in trying to decipher her outburst, I chalked the whole thing up to it being just one of her episodes. Little did I know the dime incident would explode into a full-fledged family feud.

Following our estrangement, Mom began telling anyone who would listen that Darrin and I had stolen her three precious dimes - which, by the way, she claimed were worth $10,000 apiece. According to her, Darrin and I stole her dimes in order to pay for a renovation to our home, which conveniently cost $30,000. The renovation was done to better accommodate Darrin's mother Jane, who had moved in with us for a time after she suffered a stroke and the death of her husband. She was partially paralyzed as a result of the stroke, and needed a handicap-accessible bathroom. As she was already living with us, we remodeled our downstairs bathroom to accommodate her needs. Upon hearing about this, my mother chose to paint us as "desperate"—a band of thieves willing to steal from an elderly woman in order to pay for extravagant renovations. Once again, she found a way to sit comfortably on her throne of victimization, built on fabrication and lies.

It took me ages to identify the catalyst for her outburst on the phone, and as usual, it all pointed back to her insatiable hunger for attention. She was so jealous that we were caring for Darrin's mother, and went so far as to renovate our home for her, that Mom simply couldn't stand it. My mother-in-law had been living with us for almost six months before I received the call about the dimes. Mom perceived it as abandonment, and she let the hurt fester inside her for months, before she finally snapped. It was one of the final straws that led to my decision to end the relationship.

Mom used the "stolen" dimes to justify the separation, in a way that portrayed her as a victim without fault. Many heard the story, and some even believed it – Jack being one of them. It became the cause of a years-long silent war between siblings and relatives, before Mom passed away.

25

Surprise

I have never liked surprise parties, and did not understand why for a long time. I'm not referring to surprises in general like a gift, or a thoughtful kind act, from those I love. It's surprise parties that are thrown for me that instill the feeling of fear. Personally, I could live my life happily without ever having another surprise party thrown in my honor. These events trigger panic or hypervigilance, as surprise parties are a trigger that sets off a PTSD episode.

It took some time before I could verbalize this to others because I didn't understand it myself. Surprises have a negative effect based on my experiences of the past—like the infamous 25th anniversary party—and is the case for many holidays and special occasions in my life. For most of my life, major holidays like July 4th, Christmas, Thanksgiving and Easter had to be celebrated in a specific way. Everyone would go to Mom's, she would cook for days and present us with an incredible meal at exactly twelve noon. Food that wasn't homemade was not allowed and even frowned upon. There were no concessions for in-laws, alternative plans, or different times and dates. The few times I dared to make other plans, even when they included Mom, were accepted only reluctantly and with consequences. At first she would agree resentfully and come—especially if I could get Jack to agree to join us. By the end of the day, every event would guarantee a shoe dropping moment when an argument, tantrum or outburst arose. This followed by her comment, "I will never leave my house again on a special occasion."

On my fiftieth birthday, Darrin surprised me with a party. Over one hundred people showed up for a Fourth of July bash—friends, coworkers, colleagues and several neighbors. The party was an amazing time with a DJ, dancing, swimming, and all the patriotic trimmings. Toward the middle of the event, Mom was hovering in the dining room whispering to Jack, complaining about how she was never leaving her house for another holiday and if anyone wanted to see her they would have to come to her house. When I asked her what was going on, she started with a twisted list of every word someone said and was analyzing my choice in friends. "Your nosey friend Tracey asked me when I got here, where I lived and how long I was staying. It's none of her Goddamn business, that's what I said. How dare she ask me questions? Where did you find these friends? Who does she think she is?" "Your kids believe all this shit these people are saying." "And that father-in-law of yours, he is an asshole, talking about all the work you did on this house as if it was his. This is *my* house." "I'm never leaving home again on a holiday and you will have to come there to see me." I stepped right into her roller-coaster ride as she went dramatically up and down, insulting my friends, children and in-laws and berating me for my poor taste of character. It was a quick turn from love-bombing to disparagement and control. Make no mistake, this outburst was tailored to fit her need for attention and jealousy that the focus was on me. Frustrated that the party wasn't centered around her, she felt the inherent need to take back control. It has always been hard for me to understand why she could be so mean, get so jealous, and be so competitive. I remember lying in bed that night after everyone had left, not thinking of the fun, dancing, gifts and friends by trying to control my anxiety and holding back my tears, Happy Birthday to me.

Her comment "this is my house" stemmed from when I built the house almost twenty years prior. In order to get the loan, the bank wanted to see at least $1000 in my savings account. I didn't have it so I asked Mom if I could borrow the money from her. She was more than happy to loan me the money, with interest of course. I borrowed it, and paid it back. I had no idea that this process, in her mind, gave her a portion of ownership over my house, "You would not have this house if it wasn't for me, this is my house", she so often claimed.

This was just one example of her typical antics at a family event, although she would behave so cunningly that almost no one would notice the damage she had done or brush it off by saying *oh that is just Marilyn!* In the aftermath, I would inevitably find myself in a tailspin of anxiety and fear, again silently falling victim to her manipulation. She had perfected her ability to fool me into a false sense of security, then expertly time the moment when she could pull the rug out from underneath me. This ensured an overwhelming feeling of panic and increased heart rate which I could not explain. I usually thought of it as an anxiety attack and now know it as my PTSD kicking in. Overcoming my hatred of surprises involved recalling these negative emotions and memories, which was a wildly disturbing experience. However, by consciously reminding myself that the past has no place in my present, I was able to somewhat dissolve the anxiety she created for me.

The last time I was caught off guard in this way was while reading to a gym filled with elementary school students on one of my book tours. I looked to the back of the room to see a familiar looking silver-haired woman smiling back at me. At first glance, she bore a shocking resemblance to my mother and I, in turn, felt a rush of anxiety that took my breath away. It was a frightening reaction and the mere concept of my mother showing up to one of my readings instantly propelled me to the knee-jerk fear reaction I associated with my mother. I froze in mid-sentence, similar to the opossum's reaction to being bullied in my children's book *Sticks Stones and Stumped.*

This response happens more often in children because the developmental capacity to protect themselves is markedly limited. Rational or not, a child will freeze when they feel uncared for, unloved, abandoned, or attacked. This was an all too common feeling for me as a child and for a brief second it returned. My fear quickly subsided, realizing it was actually my Aunt Gloria. Her resemblance to my mother was striking enough to subconsciously stun me. It made no sense, as I knew my aunt was there; she had come with me that morning, but irrational fear had taken over. The glance out of the corner of my eye activated the automatic "fight-flight-freeze" response. My body and mind alerted, ready for action in an instant, even though I was experiencing a nonexistent threat.

After many years, Aunt Gloria and I were finally able to bond in a way that had never been possible before severing ties with my mother, and it has been such a memorable time for us. There are no put-downs, complaints, or manipulations, just simply a loving aunt proudly observing her niece's accomplishments. I was so filled with joy, although I still worried it could be ruined if my mother showed up.

The time I spend with Aunt Gloria is the closest I come to feeling the true concern and devotion a child feels from a mother. She resembles my mother and has the same voice. It is like a dream, one where I experienced my mother as a kind, loving parent.

Each morning of the tour, Aunt Gloria would ask, "How did you sleep, dear?" and always wanted to make sure I had breakfast before we left the hotel. On the other hand, given the history I had with my mother, I was unintentionally waiting for the other shoe to drop—would she be like my mother? But I realized she never would be. I am overwhelmed with gratitude and love for my aunt, and I cherish the memories we make together. I hope she realizes how much our time together means to me and the void it has filled. I am very grateful to have her in my life again, along with all my cousins.

The newfound bond with Aunt Gloria was a surprise to us both. As she told me early on in our renewed relationship, "I was hesitant to take you back into my life, out of fear that you would hurt me like your mother did. Even my children have warned me against you—they say you might be just like her."

So many people had made this assumption. I was never given the chance to demonstrate how different I was from my mother, and as she created and spread so many rumors, nobody really knew the kind of person I truly was. Aunt Gloria was so excited to learn that these assumptions were wrong, as was I, and she invited me back into her life with unconditional love and support.

Even with time, counseling, and self-healing, I am still wary of all things unexpected. Although, there have been a few real-life shocks that I was more than happy to experience. One morning while cleaning out Mom's house after she passed away, I heard my daughter Elizabeth call out to the rest of us to come to the dining room, where she and Helen were packing up the china. They had discovered a grey steel cash box, and a paper bag containing a Ziploc bag of Kennedy half dollars; the same coins supposedly stolen during Dad's calling hours, thirty-five years earlier. As Elizabeth held up a bag of over fifty dollars-worth of coins, Darrin asked incredulously, "Didn't Marilyn say that all of her half dollars were stolen?" We all stood in shock, while the realization flooded over us like a tsunami. Jokingly, I piped up, “I don’t suppose there is a little black change purse with three dimes, is there?”

Pulling out a small leather coin purse, Elizabeth said, “Do you mean this one?”

And there they were. The infamous three dimes, supposedly a thousand times worth their face value, that Darrin and I had allegedly stolen. Nothing could have rivaled the glee I felt upon seeing Jack’s reaction. It was utterly priceless. Having fully believed Mom’s claim of our thievery, his confrontation with one of her biggest lies made me feel truly exonerated. Although I was shocked to have found them, I couldn’t wipe the smile off my face. The thirty cents worth of validation was finally found.

Everyone left the house for coffee after the discovery, but Jack and I stayed behind to clean out Mom’s desk. In doing so, we stumbled across her original notarized will in a manila envelope. Looking confused, Jack turned to me and said, "But, she told me that Darrin stole it!"

"Stole it?" I exclaimed. "How could he have stolen it?"

"She said he broke in through the sewing room window," he answered, his words dripping with chagrin.

I couldn't muster a better response than incredulity. "And you believed that?" I said, remembering that yet untrue, being a victim of thievery was a common tale of Mom's I learned to ignore. Apparently Jack did not.

After close examination, we discovered copies of all the emails I had sent to Mom, pleading with her to stop her manipulations and negative behaviors toward me and my family. There was also a revised version of her will, and there was absolutely no mention of my name. Jack was named as beneficiary and one of Mom's friends, Joyce, was named executor of the will.

Mom had always described Joyce as her "rich friend", and her "second family". Pictures of Joyce's family were ones that adorned the living room gallery and overflowed into her bedroom. In yet another twist, Mom had somehow convinced Joyce to periodically send her money, although I knew for a fact that she didn't need it. Perhaps it was Joyce's unsuspecting generosity that won her a place in the will, or maybe it was payment for a secret Mom was keeping for her. Either way, Joyce was one of a precious few who were fooled by Mom's antics. Because of her social status, Joyce would never see the true Marilyn. Her money and power was something that was too alluring to let Mom's guard down.

One particular individual who wasn't charmed by Mom's manipulations was a woman named Carol. Carol had once been the daughter-in-law of Mom's long-time boyfriend, who we called Grampa C. She was not one to mince words, and she had a wonderful way of expressing her opinion, whether her audience wanted it or not.

One day, my daughter Erica called seeking my advice, as she had started seeing Carol regularly around town – dropping off children at school, at the store, etc. Carol didn't recognize Erica, as the last time they'd seen each other Erica was a pre-teen. They were becoming more friendly with each coincidental meeting, and Erica felt the need to come forward about who she was – but was afraid it would ruin a potential friendship. We agreed that honesty was the best course of action, so the next time they ran into each other, Erica admitted that she was Marilyn's granddaughter.

Carol was visibly shocked, and actually backed away from Erica, as if she were radioactive. Erica rushed to clarify that she had no relationship with her grandmother, nor did she want one, and Carol immediately relaxed at this assurance. They continued to foster a friendship, and from it we gleaned even more stories about Marilyn's madness. One thing we learned was that whenever Carol's children did try to contact their grandfather, Mom had intervened. Whether it was intercepting calls or not passing on messages, she built an impassable roadblock between Grampa C and his grandchildren. When he died, he left everything to my mother – not that it was much, but it was a matter of principle. Because of my mother's intervening, he assumed his grandchildren didn't want him involved in their life, and he died never having the chance to say goodbye. As he lay dying in a nursing home, we were called to say good-bye and we were told by my mother that the grandchildren didn't want to come. They were never notified.

No funeral was held, because Mom said he didn't want one. She cremated him and his ashes sat on her mantle until she decided she wanted to bury him in private.

Although they didn't have any physical remains to bury, his grandchildren, stepchildren, and step-grandchildren honored him with a celebration of life, without Marilyn's involvement. Mom was furious with Carol and her daughters when she found out and cut ties with everyone else in his family that she was still in contact with.

As for Carol, when Erica told her Mom had passed, her response was simple and firm. "Good."

26

Brotherly Love

Jack was always Mom's pride and joy. She cherished him in every way, and he was lucky to have only experienced her wrath once in his sixty years. He made her pay dearly for the embarrassment it caused, and she never again lashed out at him. It was a desperate time for her, as he was transitioning into a new life, one that didn't include her. At least in his times of struggle, she was needed - but he had escaped those days, and was finally on the right track to a new life—and marriage.

I don't blame my brother for being the Chosen One, nor do I feel any animosity toward him. Mom used the same parental rearing practices she learned from her parents. Mom was the favorite child, for no particular reason other than being the youngest child after the death of a younger sibling—an immeasurable loss no parent should have to endure. She received abundant affirmation and privilege while her mother neglected the emotional needs of the other children. Mom grew up feeling powerful, entitled, believing she could do or accomplish anything, while the other Bryson children grew up working their fingers to the bone, feeling like outsiders and unimportant. Mom repeated this cycle on Jack and I.

As for Jack, I have always loved and cared for him and am thankful he didn't experience the same emotional abuse that I endured. He was oblivious to my abuse and did as he was told. However, I do feel a sense of loss at the lack of relationship we had as children - our interactions were brief and closely monitored. This was due in part to our three-year age gap, and also the significant amount of time I spent away with my grandparents. We didn't build much of a relationship until after we both left home and were well into our twenties.

We were, and still are, total opposites. Jack was athletic, and excelled in any sport he tried. He has always been handsome and charismatic—tall, blonde hair, and with striking blue eyes, like Dad. At times (when he smiles) you can see hints of Dad in his smirk. I, on the other hand, am short, with dark hair, olive skin, and brown eyes. We have no similar interests.

Jack lived with me for a short period before he married for the first time, which finally gave us the opportunity to get to know each other without the influence of our parents. To the observer, it seemed that was his motive to move in with me in the first place—but I wasn't fooled. I was sure he'd found himself in some kind of trouble, and needed a place to stay so that our mother wouldn't find out about whatever situation he'd gotten himself into. But I didn't mind, and hoped that my offer of help and a place to stay would create a stronger bond between us. Sadly, it did not.

After Mom passed away, Jack and I finally had to talk. We co-owned her house, and we had to evict her boyfriend, clean it out, and get it ready to sell. We were forced into a collaborative situation, and were both surprised to find we worked well together. Whether it was day-to-day texts, phone calls, making decisions, or cleaning and moving everything out of the house, we found ourselves comfortably working together towards our common goal.

Once we closed on the house, the comradery was over. He no longer saw the need to have me in his life. I wasn't surprised but my feelings were hurt. Excited about finally being able to have an adult sibling relationship free of interference and ultimatums from our mother was something I had always longed for, especially as Jack and his wife spend their summers three miles from my home. When nothing enticed him to visit or call, I came to realize that it was probably impossible, for the mere reason that my brother's behavior was learned and mimicked by observing Mom's treatment of me. A relationship of sixty years was not going to change because we found some common ground on one issue which was now over. My role in the relationship was to *fix* the situation. It ended there.

Toward the end of her life, when Mom and I were not speaking, she told Jack that if he spoke to me she would never talk to him again. I wonder sometimes if his loyalty to her is what made it so easy for him to cut me out of his life. Or maybe it had something to do with the final surprises he received from Mom, post mortem.

During the week of cleaning, various friends and relatives stopped by to say hello and to retrieve items from the house that they hoped to take. Two women dropped in unannounced, one inquiring about an old framed picture of Jesus promised to her by Mom's boyfriend, and the other seeking a cardboard box containing the ashes of Mom's cousin Yale, which sat on the mantle—items we were more than happy to part with.

Sue Ellen, the friend requesting the ashes, stayed for a chat at the kitchen table with Jack, Helen, and myself. She was the one friend that Mom had in the end, and a new friend of only a few years. I was curious as to why she wanted the ashes of cousin Yale, and never did get an answer. The conversation moved towards why I had not been around much in the last few years. The small-town rumor mill is an ambitious one, and the stories surrounding my estrangement from my mother had neighbors and friends wondering what instigated our mutual silence. Out of the blue, Sue Ellen inadvertently dropped the bomb, "So, your mother figured out you knew that Leo wasn't your father and assumed that's why you stopped speaking to her. Made sense to me," she concluded.

As unexpected as it was, that kind of unsolicited statement would have shocked even the most composed. We were, understandably, left in awe. "Wait," she said. "You didn't know?"

I hesitated to capture the look on Jack's face and replied, "Yes, I knew, and no, that is not why we stopped speaking." It wasn't her business, so I left it at that.

For the first time, Jack was hearing it from another source, and with a word from one loose set of lips, his whole reality changed. Jack was never impressed by my claim of false paternity. Whether he didn't believe it, or simply didn't want to, it had not been a pleasant conversation between us, but in this moment, truth burst into the empty spaces. This also gave me the answer as to why Mom did not want him to contact me. She was afraid I knew about my paternity and that I would tell Jack. She couldn't lose Jack; that would have literally killed her.

For many years, my intuition surrounding my identity sat heavy within me. Now, the house where I had been stifled and oppressed, a place I had wanted so desperately to run from, had morphed into a stage upon which the truth could be unveiled. Watching it unfold in front of me, I felt like I had just won the triple crown. First the coins, then the will, and now the icing on the cake—Mom confided in someone and the cat was out of the bag. Don't get me wrong, I wasn't gloating, I had laid out the facts before and this new information was providing my brother with the evidence to back up my claim.

After Sue Ellen left, Jack, Helen and I discussed Jack taking a DNA test to confirm if we were only half siblings. He had concerns that the test would open him up to more information than he was ready to know. I was honest with him about the risk you run when looking into your genetics—you can't be sure what you'll find. If anyone asks my opinion on taking a recreational DNA test to look into their heritage, I have a much stronger, informed opinion now than I did when I took my first test. I would never recommend it without a warning label. One must be ready for the unknown, as it may not turn out the way it is portrayed in ads and commercials. Genealogy is a Pandora's box and is full of things you can't take back, information you might not have bargained for. Most importantly, you're laying bare other people's secrets.

The Lost Family: Your Genes Are Not Yours Alone by Libby Copeland is a great book and resource to help guide the decision on whether to take a test, and contains information on how best to process the results. Had I read this book before unpacking my own genealogy, I may have been better equipped and prepared to digest the results. I wish I had more knowledge before I started this journey; it would have given me insight in many different ways and maybe help me absorb the results easier.

Jack was smart to be concerned. One of the stories I anticipated that might be uncovered was that we would find out the truth of Dad's paternity, that he had not been the biological son of Pepere. It was probably too soon for Jack to absorb that idea. With all the difficulty he had in believing my stories, and the shock he may experience learning we were only half siblings, any more surprises may have been just too much for him.

Oblivious to the bomb she may have dropped before she left, Sue Ellen meandered on to a story about Mom's love for fried clams, and her favorite restaurant, Anglers, where she and her boyfriend Mick dined frequently. She claimed the staff loved Mom and had posted a shrine in her memory. We laughed, thinking it was a stretch of a story, but after a long day and the serious talk, we figured we would check it out.

The Log Cabin restaurant, now Anglers, was always a favorite of mine growing up. A Newport Maine staple for over fifty years, the log decor and warm stone fireplace sets a cozy atmosphere for patrons. Being a cold November night we opted for a booth close to the fireplace, where we could honor our mother by ordering some of her favorite foods. Out of the corner of my eye, I noticed a framed photo on the mantle. It was Mom and one other person, the owner. Jack, Helen and I agreed, this must be what Sue Ellen was talking about.

When the waitress came to serve us I asked, "Can you tell me why there is a photo of our mother on your mantle?"

The waitress was overjoyed and began to tear up. "You are Marilyn's children? Oh my, let me tell the girls," and within seconds the entire wait staff was crowded around the booth. "We loved your mother," one said. "She was so funny and kind to us, what a character! You have to come see our poster."

We followed the waitstaff to the adjoining room, where a wall was covered with a collage of photos of Mom with staff and patrons, as if she was a celebrity.

I wasn't surprised, only amused. I had seen it many times—the covert narcissist's insidious behavior to trap a victim. Displayed on the wall was Mom's craving for admiration. How could someone who was unable to show empathy to her own daughter, behave in such a loving way toward others? No one has been able to answer this question; there is only speculation for the disorder. But here she was, the star of the show and the waitstaff, her audience and fans. I shrugged my shoulders and accepted that the waitstaff knew and remembered Mom in a totally different light, it wasn't my place to ruin that image for them. Although it was so far from the person I knew, it fit with what Jack had known for his sixty years.

27

Friends or Minions

Mom usually couldn't have more than a few main characters in the dramatic show of life at one time, as it was all she could juggle. Her magic number was usually three. With more than three, mistakes were made that caused stress and chaos. When I was young, it was my dad, brother Jack and whoever else was the guest star of the day: a friend, Aunt Bert, Nana and on rare occasions, me. When Dad passed, she inserted another man and Jack always held the firm number one spot. The third person was interchangeable. When I was able to escape there were others who took my place as her third person. One was our family friend, Janice.

In her seventies, Mom was diagnosed with breast cancer; a small lump under her arm that was determined to be cancerous. She needed to have a lumpectomy, but did not need chemotherapy. The doctors suggested a few rounds of radiation as a precautionary measure. I would drive up to her house, take her to the doctors and return home in one day. Because of the weekly appointments and me living far away, Janice stepped in to help. Jack was not available; he couldn't take time off from his job.

Mom tried to justify why she had cancer. According to her, it had nothing to do with sixty years of smoking, family history or thirty years of taking estrogen replacement. Her conclusion was that Grampa C used to poke her in the breast with his finger, which caused the cancer. "It was his Alzheimer's," she would say. We didn't bother to argue the point.

When Mom was diagnosed, Grampa C had already passed away and she was living alone. A few years prior to his passing, Mom had a growing concern that he was showing signs of Alzheimer's or dementia. She called his son Rob, Carol's ex-husband. Mom was hoping Rob and I could help get Grampa C to see a specialist. Mom described him as declining rapidly and wanted him seen as soon as possible. Needless to say, we were all very concerned with what we were hearing. He was a sweet, kind man and a loving step-grandfather to Liam and Quinn.

We made an appointment with one of the best neurologists in Southern Maine and Grampa C went through a series of comprehensive tests over a period of weeks. Rob and I sat with Mom as she listed all the symptoms he was exhibiting and concerns for her ability to physically care for him. Mom wanted him to have treatment then and there, but the doctor refused until his evaluation was complete. When we returned for the last consultation, the doctor was concerned and direct. The test results and patient interview did not match any of the symptoms Mom had explained. Rob and I were shocked to hear that there were no signs of any dementia or Alzheimer's. It was true that Grampa C would sometimes forget people, usually students he knew from being a principal, but they were kids when he knew them, and he didn't recognize them as adults. The doctor was annoyed to say the least and very honest in his assessment. "Mr. C shows no signs of Alzheimer's or dementia," he confirmed.

We left the office with Mom muttering, "That doctor is a quack, he doesn't live with us and see what I see every day, he doesn't know anything—educated fool is what he is." A few weeks later, Mom asked Grampa C to leave and made arrangements for him to move to Florida with his step daughter. She then moved her cousin Yale into the house, and into her bedroom.

It was a sorrowful circumstance for such a great man, although Grampa C never challenged Mom, and allowed the gaslighting to happen, even confessing to the doctor that he had none of the symptoms she claimed. He left, and within a week was begging to come home. He missed her so much, and longed for the place he had lived all his life. Mom finally agreed after a couple of months to allow his return, with conditions, of course. The main condition was he would return to the spare bedroom.

Grampa C had a master's degree in education, and a forty-year career as a principal, not to mention he was a well-respected community member, yet he was willing to believe that certain incidents were happening to him. He was deeply destabilized as a victim and began to doubt his ability to see the world as it truly was. He believed that he might have Alzheimer's, if Mom said he did. But Mom's goal as the gaslighter was to rid him from her life for her personal gain. She successfully convinced him to question his own mental and physical stability. It was one of the most subtly calculated gaslighting situations I have ever observed. Rob and his new wife had little to do with Mom after this happened. Rob didn't try to free his dad; he was a grown man and his life was his to live so they decided to stay silent. This gave me deep insight and clarity as to what my own father must have experienced.

Based on the story of Grampa C, it was pointless to argue with Mom when she went on about him causing the cancer, there was no use. I was silent, and the surgeon said nothing, just looked at us and shook his head.

At the time of her surgery and treatment, Janice was taking Mom to the doctors and to radiation therapy most of the time. She was extremely helpful and was present with us the day we met with the surgeon. Janice had been a family friend since she was a very young girl, and our parents were friends.

As a little girl, I remember, wishing I could be just like her. She was five years older than me and was beautiful, popular, and had the best clothes, hair, and makeup. She would bring clothes to my mother to tailor for her and I would be in awe of her presence and style.

Many times, Janice would take my place as the daughter, but in a different way than one would expect.

Once Janice's parents passed, my mother jumped in as a surrogate mother and friend; mind you, Janice was an adult at the time. She confided in Mom, and was instantly caught in the web without any acknowledgement of the invitation and conditions. While mourning her parents and dealing with her own issues, Mom invited her into the web-house for a visit. Janice found comfort in their friendship and would take her shopping and to appointments, even though Mom had no physical ailments prohibiting her to drive herself; this was a setup for the future.

With Janice in her circle, I was no longer needed. Janice became the third person. If Mom would have a falling out with Janice, she would be relegated to the back burner, and I was returned as the third person. When that happened, Janice didn't understand the cold shoulder and questioned herself on what she did wrong to desire Mom's cold shoulder.

Janice and I were always kept in separate compartments, not to socialize or talk; we could only assume and make decisions on the stories we were being fed. My appreciation for her beauty and personality was used as ammunition in Mom's game. Mom had a brilliant knack of playing people against each other without them knowing. Living two hours away, I didn't pay attention to what was going on in my hometown. If I was visiting, then others were not invited, lest my mother's games be exposed.

By compartmentalizing us, no one could compare stories. If and when I spoke with Janice, Mom would want to be present, in order to control the conversation. She would also quiz and prepare me with topics if Janice or anyone was visiting during my stay. It was done in a cunning and believable way. "Poor Janice is coming down, don't say anything about her drinking, she doesn't like to talk about it and I don't want her to get mad at me for telling you her secret," she confided to me.

Ironically, when Mom was going through her cancer treatment, Janice and I found we had many things to discuss and a significant amount of time to talk privately. We surprisingly shared a lot of stories.

Previously, Mom told me not to call Janice after 4 p.m., warning that she was an alcoholic who started drinking in the afternoon and would be too drunk to talk. Honestly, I didn't know her as an adult and wasn't familiar with her situation so I took it as gospel. The idea of her driving mom to her appointments hit the top of my concern list, but I guess all was fine, given Mom's appointments were in the morning hours. The real story was different. Four p.m. was when Janice ended her day as a home health care consultant and when her husband arrived home from work. Why the story? It was Mom's tool to keep us away from each other so we didn't compare notes, because it was fun for her, and most importantly so she could maintain control.

The story started to unfold when Mom, Janice and I were sitting in the exam room after checking Mom in for her day surgery. The doctor came in to talk with us, and he unknowingly lit a fuse. We were anxious for his approach, anticipating the conversation would be tense, as surgical conversations most often are. We had no idea what we were in for and wanting to address the family, he asked the question, "Which one of you is Marilyn's daughter?"

"I am," I answered, in unison with my mother as Mom blurted out, "She is." The only problem was, she wasn't pointing at me.

It didn't matter that it was a serious moment, Mom was Mom, and her antics never changed. It never got any less embarrassing, but we were able to quickly recover after a brief moment of shock and refocus our attention on the task at hand, right after we cleared up the confusion. Again, in unison, Janice and I pointed at each other and said, "Friend and daughter." Janice continued, "I am like a daughter to her," with a response back from Mom, "They are both my daughters." Frustrated by this and the Grampa C story, the doctor just addressed us both and explained how the day would go.

Janice and I went to a local restaurant to have lunch while we waited for word that the surgery was over and Mom was safely back in recovery. It was an informative lunch, to say the least. We started to exchange stories, and soon uncovered many lies and inconsistencies. Our previously guarded relationship started to turn into an alliance. We were both pawns in Mom's chess game; two intelligent women, mothers, wives, and self-employed business women conned by the master. More importantly, Janice discovered that I was not a neglectful daughter and I learned that she was not an alcoholic! The stories we shared were therapeutic. Mom was the puppet master and we were only some of the hanging fools that bought into her puppetry. The stories were not outrageous, just lies.

We both were able to take the upper hand in the situation moving forward by staying in contact and comparing notes, although we never let my mother know. Communication became key for us. As we started confiding in each other, we were able to understand and somewhat heal or commiserate with each other. There were no reason to concoct these stories other than for control and pleasure.

Janice and Mom had been estranged for some time when she got the news that Mom had passed away. Wanting some peace, Janice called the funeral home to ask if she could have a private visit, and they in turn called to tell me. She couldn't visit the body, as Mom had already been sent for cremation, and in any case, they would not allow it without Jack's approval. I called Janice and asked her why she had requested a private visit.

Her response was simple, she needed closure and wanted to say her final words. Words to tell Mom, the friend that abused her for years, what she really thought of her, now that Mom couldn't respond back.

Janice was not the only friend that broke ties with Mom. There were many. Penny was another. She was a friend that lived across the rainbow-colored stream in front of our houses for many years. When I was younger I used to babysit for her three children and our families were good friends.

Penny, a sweet, kind woman by nature, was a neighbor, friend, and Mom's coworker at one point. Like Janice, Penny and Mom share many stories that could fill a book and play out the same way. I didn't see or hear from her after Mom passed away, however she showed up at the private burial eleven months later, which she was duped into attending by Mom's boyfriend, Mick. She was embarrassed and apologetic for showing up to see only six people at the grave site. This uncomfortable event took us into a series of conversations about their demised relationship.

Penny was there for the same reason Janice asked to see Mom post mortem. She needed to silently say her piece. I found out that after forty plus years of friendship, Penny had finally got up enough courage to confront Mom and end the relationship. The final altercation that led to cutting her ties made Penny uncomfortable confessing, and I gave my word not to repeat it. What was interesting was what happened in the aftermath of the break-up. In a heated phone call, Penny anxiously explained that she didn't want Mom to ever contact her again. It was easier over the phone, as she could hang up. Mom did not call back, however she went to visit Penny's daughter,

Melissa, at her office the next day with a parting gift. Mom returned a box of lipstick Penny had given her. "I'm returning the lipstick that Penny gave me, would you give it to her?" Mom asked her.

Melissa took the box and gave it to her mother. When the women opened the box, they discovered that each tube of lipstick was broken, destroyed or crumbled. This was a typical harsh and common display of Mom's revenge. Penny was distraught, and that was the reaction Mom was hoping for.

28

The Insatiable Appetite of the Narcissist

Eventually, my mother's bizarre moods and tumultuous personality started to leak out of the home. Whispers in the community could be heard, and grew as she got older, especially after Dad and Grampa C passed away. At least when Dad was alive, he would deter her inappropriate or demeaning behavior by gently saying, "Now Marilyn, is that true"? He would quietly interrupt and change the subject just like a dog herding cattle. It was an illusion though, she never really got worse, it only appeared that way as the men were no longer around to be her buffer, reigning her back to reality.

I started to see how she tested her behavior outside of the home, trying it out on more and more people as her intimate audience dwindled. When we all lived together, Mom locked the secrets of her mental health and disorders securely inside the walls of our home, creating a toxic air she spilled willingly over her choice victims, particularly her sister and I. With no one there to monitor, combined with the inability to get much needed continual supply of attention, Mom was provoked to go to further extremes to feed her narcissistic and sociopathic appetite.

Mom's insatiable appetite for attention and admiration mimicked that of a vampire, sucking me dry at any opportunity. It was clear she hated seeing me happy or successful, taking advantage of special moments in my life to ruin the occasion.

When my first children's book, *Sticks, Stones, and Stumped* was published, it was an exciting occasion for me. I remember the books arriving at my house, I was surrounded by my creation of several months of hard work, and it hit the best seller list on Amazon the first day.

I presented my mother with a copy in the fashion of showing a newborn for the first time, "look at what I did and what I have". I had worked over a year to lobby for harassment and bullying prevention laws in the state, wrote a book, and was now on a book tour.

Subconsciously, I was thinking, "tell me I am a good girl and I've done a great job, Mommy". She took the book and set it aside with a slight toss on the kitchen table and went on to talk about herself. No matter what I did, I couldn't squeeze out positive attention. Not to say she wouldn't brag about me to others to show off her accomplishments, but she never gave that to me.

Whether she read it or not, I don't know, she didn't open it while I was there. I did ask her later what she thought and she responded, "I don't know, I haven't had time to look at it."

After her death, I found the book, along with the ceramic homemade 25th anniversary plate engraved with the wrong year, stuffed in a bottom drawer in the bathroom under all the old Christmas decorations. I thought it interesting that she placed the two significant gifts from me in the same place, literally as far away as she possibly could in the house, instead of just throwing them away or destroying them. It wasn't her intention to keep them as mementos, it was done so that someday I would find them in such an insignificant place.

The same week I gave Mom my book, I was presenting at a nearby school with my son Liam in tow. I invited Mom, Grampa C, and my Aunt Bert to come to the general assembly to hear us both address the students. After the general assembly, they joined Liam and I in the classroom. My aunt was so proud. It was her home town and she told everyone I was her favorite niece. The family sat amongst the children and teachers in the gym as I talked about being kind and respectful to others and reading the book to an engaged group of grammar school students.

After the general assembly, we made visits to each classroom. We engaged in a project that required the students to trace their hand on a piece of paper and write down five words that would help them remember to be kind to one another. Drawing a large oversized hand on the chalkboard, I collected the papers and wrote the children's words on each finger.

Mom thought it would be fun to play as well. As I was writing the words on the chalkboard and discussing positive character traits with the students, I was taken aback by a paper that showed an adult's hand with long red fingernails. All the words written were slang or four-letter words. Slut, whore, bitch, snob, know-it-all and profanity too disgusting to repeat—you get the picture. As I looked up at her, she smiled with an evil, Cheshire Cat grin. She then got up and left in the middle of my presentation, steering Aunt Bert and Grampa C. quickly out of the classroom.

After the school visit, I confronted Mom on her behavior and she responded, "Oh, I'm sorry, I thought you wanted me to write down things we shouldn't say about you."

Yes, that was exactly what I wanted to write on the chalkboard for the second graders, blasphemous and obscene language, I thought. Of course, that was not her intent, because she never established, exhibited or taught us moral behaviors and at that moment she was reminding me who was in charge. There were no boundaries, everything was fair play and this was the perfect opportunity for her to cunningly play her cards, collect her winnings and leave the table.

29

Adoption: Another Word for Love

In the early 1990's, Darrin and I were in Orlando for a medical conference. We were overjoyed with the knowledge that I was carrying a child, not long after I had my first miscarriage, and we thought a little vacation was in order. The day before Darrin left for home (I would stay longer for the conference), we leisurely explored EPCOT, strolling from country to country in a daze. We even bought a woven baby basket, like the one Moses was found in, handmade in Morocco. Darrin carried it around with him all day and brought it back on the plane the next morning. A few hours after his plane took off, and with only a few days left of my trip, I miscarried for the second time.

Miscarriages are vastly misunderstood by society as a whole, and are rarely openly discussed. Women suffer in solitude, mourning the baby that was viscerally real to them while bystanders wonder why they cry for a child that was never held. Each time I became pregnant, the baby growing inside of me was as real to me as anyone else I could reach out and touch.

After my second miscarriage, I cried for days – so much so that my eyes swelled shut. Seeing this, Darrin was understandably hesitant for us to keep trying to get pregnant, but we were both determined to have a child.

During the time I was home recovering, a friend and colleague who had vast knowledge of infertility, reached out to offer his support. I'll never forget the words he shared with me.

"You have half the battle conquered by getting pregnant. Don't give up, find a reason that you are not staying pregnant," he said.

Pondering his words, I realized that each miscarriage had occurred in the same week of my pregnancy. Then it hit me – a memory from years ago, a case I had become familiar with while working as an administrator for an obstetrics and gynecological practice. The patient, a woman in her late thirties, kept having miscarriages at the same week of her pregnancies due to a low level of progesterone – she was perimenopausal. She was prescribed progesterone suppositories and bed rest for the first twenty weeks of her pregnancy. I presented my findings to my husband and obstetrician, excited and emboldened by my discovery. The physician was more easily convinced than Darrin, but in the end we decided to give it a try. In tandem with the progesterone suppositories, we would also reopen the adoption process. It was our Hail Mary.

While we made the necessary preparations for an adoption, I began with the regimen of progesterone and checking my temperature each morning to track ovulation. Not the most romantic process, I'll admit. We also worked with the state to become foster parents, which was required for the time period between birth and private adoption. I was so consumed with the adoption process, I realized one morning that I had neglected to take my temperature for several days, and as a result had missed the window for conception. I remember standing in the bedroom crying, upset that we missed our opportunity, and Darrin, so calm and level headed, reassuring me that we would still have another chance.

A few weeks later, I was standing alongside my luggage, ready to leave for Texas, holding the pregnancy test and failing to contain my excitement. I was pregnant again. It was my first time traveling since the trip to Orlando, and I was feeling understandably anxious. Now a woman of thirty-nine and reeling from two miscarriages, I was coming to terms with the idea that I might never carry another baby. Adding to this, only six weeks prior we had lost a baby in a failed adoption process. However, as I've said before, I rarely take no for an answer – and this situation was no different. I had to find an answer; a solution to the problem before me. And with that, I left for Texas to meet Baby One, with Baby Two already safely within me.

On the advice of our attorney in Maine, given our parameters for adoption, we advertised in the EL Paso Weekly Shopper, a free publication in the Texas border town. We also hired an attorney in El Paso, on the advice of the Maine adoption agency, to represent us should someone respond to the ad. The day after the ad was published, I received a call. It was a girl named Maria. We both had so many questions for each other, and after our conversation I urged her to see our attorney in El Paso. She went that very day.

Maria claimed the father of her unborn child was a man named Jorge, who she had been living with until recently, and was the father of her son Jay. After meeting with the attorney, Maria asked Jorge to relinquish his rights to the unborn child so that she could travel to Maine, give birth in secret, and give the baby up for a private adoption. While speaking to him at the garage where he worked, he flatly denied his involvement in the conception of the child and claimed he wanted no part in her games. Ashamed and alone, Maria decided to change her story.

The new story she told involved a one-night-stand with a man whose name she couldn't recall, who she met while traveling through New Mexico. She had no idea how to find him, and didn't even know where he was from. However, she was adamant that this man in New Mexico was the father of the unborn child. Although the story was shaky at best, our lawyers assured us that the adoption process would be legal and safe.

Walking into the shared hotel room in downtown Dallas, my eyes were immediately drawn to the beautiful little boy sitting serenely on the bed. His wavy hair was so jet-black that the light almost reflected off it, and his twinkling brown eyes took in my arrival with interest.

His name was Joaquin, nicknamed Jay, and his even more beautiful mother Maria sat next to him, brushing her long hair. She smiled in relief when I introduced myself, and she stood up to hug me, pregnant belly protruding from her 19-year old body. The anticipation of meeting her in person had been building for weeks, and even though we had been speaking regularly over the phone and email, I still found myself existing as if in a dream, afraid to admit that this was finally happening. The thought of finally hugging my baby flashed through my brain and I felt the last 7 months of roller coaster emotions swell in my throat.

Six weeks after our first meeting in Dallas, Liam was born in Maine when I was two months pregnant with Quinn. We were prone to believe Maria's original story of the birth father, until we saw our Liam. A healthy eight-pound baby, Liam had alabaster skin and light-blue eyes that didn't hold any similarities to his brown-eyed, dark skinned Hispanic mother from Juárez, nor did he look at all like the photos of his (potential) biological father and brother. Other than his Hispanic heritage, we knew almost nothing about his genetic background. This forced us to wonder about the legitimacy of Maria's story – was Liam's biological father really some stranger from New Mexico, as she had claimed?

Given his alabaster skin and blue-eyes, we were left with the obvious conclusion that Maria's Hispanic boyfriend couldn't have been the father. We chose to believe that Liam was the child of the unknown man Maria had met in New Mexico. At that time, DNA testing wasn't commercially available, and we really didn't give it much thought, especially since she didn't know what the man's name was. We were over the moon with our baby boy and didn't revisit the issue until 20 years later, when home DNA tests became recreationally popular.

30

Truth Be Told

Liam has always known the truth about his adoption. When he was young, we would read stories to him before bed explaining how Quinn came from my belly, and Liam came from my heart. Darrin and I decided early on that hiding the truth would serve no good.

As he grew up and started asking questions, we slowly gave Liam the information he needed to understand his own birth story. Darrin and I wanted to give him everything he needed to develop a positive sense of his own identity, and a sense of well-being and self-esteem.

Adopted children often have many questions about their birth, and Liam was no different. When he asked, we always answered honestly, usually while putting him to bed at night or cuddled up at story time. One memory I hold dear from these stories was while we were vacationing in Costa Rica, when Liam was about 10 years old. Darrin and Quinn were fast asleep in one bed, after a long day of exploring the city of Liberia and chasing lizards by the pool, Fanta soda in hand.

Liam and I were snuggled in the other bed discussing the day when he started asking more questions about his adoption. He was so curious and attentive, hanging on every word, craving even the smallest of details. As an adoptive parent, the subject is one to take seriously, but the intensity of the moment was broken when a giant bug bit me on my big toe. I burst out of bed like a firecracker, hopping on one foot. We both laughed, and trying not to wake Darrin and Quinn, I continued with the story until we both drifted off to sleep. The story I told him that night wasn't anything different from what I had told him before, but he continued to ask for retellings, and Darrin and I indulged each and every time. We wanted Liam's developmental process to be built on a foundation of honesty, trust, love, and support. This would allow him to meld his birth story into his emerging identity. We wanted to provide him with continuity and consistency. We were determined to eliminate any need for him to question his history, or his sense of belonging.

In 2014, at the height of the new ancestry-testing phenomenon, we decided to run a DNA test on Liam, who was now twenty and a college student. One part of Liam's history was still absent: his biological father. Although we knew his maternal history well, we didn't have much information about the paternal side. Both of Maria's parents were in their early forties when Liam was born, and as far as Maria knew, there were no medical issues in her family. We decided to dig deeper, and purchased a DNA test through Ancestry.com.

The results of Liam's test confirmed that he was thirty-eight percent Native American, forty-one percent Spanish, and the other twenty percent a mixture of European and African descent. This last part is consistent with the history of slaves that survived the journey to the Americas centuries past.

Through these results we were able to find some of Liam's relatives, including a paternal aunt. Although she was estranged from Liam's biological father, and a half-sister by relation, she was able to help us connect the missing pieces and confirm that Jorge, Maria's boyfriend, was indeed Liam's biological father. Although Jorge had refused to acknowledge his paternity, DNA does not lie.

I had the opportunity to communicate with his aunt and his paternal grandmother several times following our discovery. With their help, we were able to gain more clarity. Liam's biological paternal grandmother and great-grandmother were both from Durango, Mexico, and were both born with white skin and blue eyes – although being 100% Hispanic. This explained our confusion when Liam was born with such fair skin. The great-grandmother was still alive, well into her nineties, and was in good health. Just like that, Liam's biological mystery was solved.

Liam's DNA test opened the door to another story I hadn't thought about in years. A story meant to be forgotten, whispered about in hushed tones, revolving around sixty years of secrets, misplaced anger, and shame. The mystery surrounding Liam's conception and the secrets kept by his birth mother was an eerie foreshadowing of my own life, a blindside I never saw coming.

31

The Blindside

When we first began talking about DNA testing, Liam's then-girlfriend and now wife, Holly, agreed with the idea that it might be fun for her to take a recreational DNA test as well. After all, her mother and I shared the same last name of Bolduc, and our families came from the same area in southwestern Québec. I was excited to think that I could be related to Holly. She has been part of our family since she and Liam started dating as freshmen in high school. She was and is like a daughter to me, and I live in constant admiration of the love and commitment she and my son share. In my opinion, it would just be icing on the cake if we found out she and I were distant cousins – we even joked that my grandchildren could also be my cousins! We laughed about the possibility and the irony of it all. I mean, really, how many Bolducs could there be from that area of Québec? We had to be linked, somehow.

For what felt like months, I waited impatiently for our test results to arrive. Liam's results arrived first, but the others took a few weeks longer. When Liam's results arrived, I had expected them to say he was Hispanic – I was not prepared to see how far back in his DNA history went, and was intrigued to know about his Native American and Spanish descent.

My results were next to arrive, and the work of interpreting them began – which was significantly more confusing than I had anticipated. The results didn't seem to match up with the history I had received from family stories. I set out to learn how to read the confusing results, and it took significant research.

I was confident that my test would come back 100% European descent. I assumed about 50% Irish and Scottish from my mother's side, and 50% French from my father's. As for Holly, we assumed she would be about 50% French as well, which turned out to be true – no surprises for her. Comparing our results, we in fact are not biologically related, nor does she share DNA with any of the Bolducs in my family. My disappointment was overshadowed by the shock of my own results, revealing to me that I was not, in fact, French.

The test revealed that I am European, as expected. The breakdown of 98% European was 49% Italian/Southern Europe and 49% Irish/British and a few other areas in Asia. I was expecting 49% Irish/Scottish, and I could understand the small percentage of Asian background. However, the 49% Italian was beyond my comprehension. I had no idea how to begin interpreting this result, as I had spent my entire life with the belief that I was French. Was my Dad's family really from Italy and had migrated into France, before relocating to Québec? That must be it, I thought, and I tried to convince myself that was the story. But then again, the odds that both sides of my paternal grandparents were originally from Italy, then all moved to

France before migrating to Canada, was statistically improbable.

I believed my whole life, up to that point, that I was French Canadian. Summer vacations were spent in Thetford Mines, a small city of 25,000 people in south-central Québec, where all the Bolduc relatives mined asbestos (except my great uncle, who was a monk in the Catholic church). How could it be, that one day in my sixties, it would all change?

Looking into a mirror, I stared at what seemed to be an unknown woman from a parallel universe. *Who am I? I thought.* Mother, daughter, sister, grandmother—I was there in the reflection, and was real, but it didn't feel that way. It felt like my whole life had been a fabrication.

I felt that I had never fit in with my family or childhood community, but I never once went down the road of questioning the legitimacy of my father. Yes, I had sometimes wondered why I didn't resemble any of my father's family, and there had been whispers and hints sprinkled in over the years. Still, I had never ventured down the path of biological research. Emotions began pouring out of me like an overflowing water basin, shock and confusion blurring my eyes. Then the tiny pieces of my life that had never added up, never felt cohesive, began to make sense. Memories of my childhood bubbled up; I was remembering all the years I felt lost and misplaced. My intuition, even as a little girl, was legitimate.

Then I remembered the discussion I had with my father that day behind the farmhouse, about men being gentlemanlike. It hadn't been about respect for my husband at the time; he was preparing me, softening the blow of what he felt to be the inevitable realization that he was not my blood relation. I revelled in his sacrifice, the decision he made to raise me as his own, the whole time knowing of Marilyn's deceit and her biggest lie.

32

Spitting Out the Truth

Once I was past the shock and able to process the idea of my newly discovered heritage, I was faced with a whole new challenge. How do I get answers to this new puzzle?

Darrin and I agreed that asking my estranged mother for clarification would be a fool's errand. That conversation would inevitably lead to "why are you trying to make trouble? Ancestry.com is out to get me – they want to take my money"! or something along these lines. Looking to her for answers would most likely leave me more frustrated and angrier than I already was. I decided to ask one of my paternal cousins to take an Ancestry DNA test. If she was related to me in any way, then it would confirm my blood relation to my father. If not, then I would be a Non-Parent Expected, (NPE), a relatively new term for individuals who discover that the man or woman that raised them, in fact, was not biologically their parent. At this point I was still living in denial, grasping madly at the hope that there was a logical explanation for my test results.

The odds were not in my favor, as the estimated percentage of the population that are NPE is between 17-32%, there was a pretty good chance I would now become part of this statistic.

My cousin Leah, six years my senior, bears a striking resemblance to my paternal grandmother Marietta. She is a true Bolduc, and there was no doubt about her biological father or grandmother. She gladly accepted my request and a test was delivered to her while I waited, not so patiently, for eight weeks before receiving any results.

On a Sunday morning in November, I received an email from Ancestry that there was a match – but it was not for me. It was for Liam, alerting him to a new distant cousin the database had been found. Disappointed, I logged on to view the updated list of family members, and saw that Leah had indeed received her results, only, she wasn't listed as a biological member of my family.

Her results had arrived several weeks prior, and I hadn't been notified because her DNA bore no similarities to my own. I was devastated.

The truth was like lidocaine on my cognitive function, numbing me from head to toe. I sank into the couch, frozen in thought while I let the realization flood through me. I am the child of some unknown man. Ever since receiving my original test, I had been holding fast to the hope that there was some obvious explanation – but the hope had been draining for weeks with each door that closed in front of me. Adding insult to injury, that very day was the anniversary of my dad's death.

I don't know how long I sat there in disbelief, unable to even shed a tear. Thoughts raced through my head as my life flashed before my eyes. Pieces started to fall in and out of place. I recounted them again; the 25th wedding anniversary, feelings of my mother always resenting me, and her bizarre pregnancy stories. My dad hinting what a true gentleman should be. And then it hit me like a ton of bricks. Dad retreated, and let Mom do as she pleased; I was her possession and she had dibs. He knew the truth whether they actually discussed it or not. Mom was fixated on my birth story for an entirely different reason than what I thought. This explained the joyous birth of Jack and the convoluted story of mine. Mom believed Jack to be the saviour of her marriage, just in case she needed it. He was the spare, bringing her peace and safety. It was at that moment I found the missing pieces to the birth puzzle and Mom's relationship with each member of our family of four.

When I recovered my powers of speech, I immediately called my Aunt Gloria to tell her the truth she had questioned for years. True to the gossip shared between sisters, my mother had indeed gone to Aunt Myra's house one night, accompanied by her "Italian friend", to use the upstairs bedroom.

I then asked Aunt Gloria if she could call her sister Myrna, now ninety-five years old, to ask if she remembered any details of that night – maybe a name, a hometown, anything. Aunt Gloria let out a heavy sigh. "Oh, Debbie, I'm so sorry, your Aunt Myrna died last week in a nursing home in Florida."

Everyone was gone, and time was not on my side. Aunt Gloria couldn't confirm anything, she only had what she knew as gossip.

The next several months were a stalling period as I continued to absorb my new reality. It was oddly similar to how I felt as a pregnant fifteen-year-old renouncing her church, faith, and family. The spiritual disconnect I experienced so many years before was the closest thing I could compare to my current feelings; a deep emptiness and loss of identity.

Darrin and I discussed the possibility of hiring a private investigator, but we had startlingly few leads. I started making a list of all the people I could remember my mother mentioning—friends from high school, acquaintances from before she was married and reaching out to distant relatives on Ancestry.com. I wrote down all the stories Mom told of her high school days, trying to jog my memory for clues. Some days I questioned whether I really wanted to know the truth, but I knew my curiosity would never abate until I solved the mystery. The possibility of redefining my heritage was a strong enough motivator to help me push past the rejection and dead ends that kept multiplying. And multiply they did. It took years to compile the map which led me to the final conclusion.

One of the most difficult aspects of this process was the betrayal I felt for my father. Why should I spend so much time searching for a man with whom I shared DNA, while

I had been raised by a man who knew the truth all along and did the job for him? I felt I was disrespecting his memory by digging into my mother's extramarital activities. Still, curiosity motivated me to keep investigating. Most of my leads turned into dead ends, and many of the people I spoke to couldn't remember details, nor were there any close relatives listed on Ancestry.com. I made almost no progress until after Mom passed away, at which point I was able to go through her old paperwork and photos, and from this I was able to connect faces with the names of old boyfriends she had in high school, but none were the "Italian boyfriend" she had mentioned several times in the past.

Just before Mom started dating my dad, she had two long term boyfriends. One of them she ended up dating again and living with after my dad passed away, but I knew it wasn't him. Freddy wasn't Italian although he had many stories to share when I tracked him down. I promised not to repeat any of his stories as they didn't relate to my paternity. The one plus side of this journey was that I was searching for an Italian man in the midst of a predominantly Irish and French population – an easy task, one might think. Once the lead with Freddy was exhausted, I tracked the second of the two boyfriends, a man named Ray.

Ray, by the letters found after Mom's death, was the true love of her life. It had to be him. I was sure of it. They had dated in her senior year of high school before he went into the military prior to Mom meeting Dad. Conveniently, he had been home on leave around the same time I was conceived. The paper trail he left led me straight to his front door, only to find he was deceased. He did, however, have three sons all living in the same area.

From our research, we were able to find the contact information for one of Ray's sons and decided to call him. The call did not go well. The man was irate, accusing us of trying to con him and take his money. He, in turn, contacted his brother Roland, to tell him of the incident. From this interaction, Darrin and I both assumed this route would also be a dead end.

To my surprise, I received a call from Roland's wife, Sally, a few weeks later. Being from the same town, Sally knew Aunt Gloria and called her for my number. Unlike the first brother I spoke to, Roland and Sally thought I might be on to something. The timeline fit, and as Sally informed me, she had also recently discovered that she was not the biological daughter of the man that had raised her. She was sympathetic for my journey and thought I deserved to know the truth. She convinced her husband to take an Ancestry.com DNA test to be sure.

While I waited for another set of test results, I spoke to Sally several times. She had been very close to Ray when he was alive, and he would tell her stories of all the good times in high school with his then girlfriend, Marilyn. He portrayed them as being quite the party couple, who were similar in personality. Sally confirmed that Ray had been home from bootcamp the month I was conceived, so it seemed we were on the right track. The only thing missing was the Italian heritage—Roland wasn't familiar with his father's full ancestry.

I romanticized that Ray and Marilyn were madly in love, and because he was away in the military, she panicked about her pregnancy –marrying the next man to come along. Roland's test results confirmed that was just a pipe dream, as Ray was not my biological father.

Turning secrets and discoveries to truths was a much needed, healing exercise. I was on the road to a long overdue answer to a question I never asked, and for another one I asked almost every day of my life: *who is my biological father* and *why doesn't my mother love me?* The DNA test gave me part of the answer to both questions and helped me understand the similarity of the two questions.

My life was an emotional map that was leading nowhere, only dead-end roads with no signs for direction. I felt like a mouse in a maze, running in circles chasing an escape route I wasn't sure I would find. Although I didn't know how I would do it, I continued my plan to escape from the maze understanding that familial toxicity is something children don't discover until they reach adulthood. It is such a difficult, hidden, self-blaming psychological situation that it actively resists being uncovered— and I was now getting the answers to untangle my reality. It was a lonely process, because above everything, Mom denied everything—to protect herself from feelings of shame, and to protect her self-perceived social status, and to justified her maltreatment of me. Habitually projected her own shortcomings on to me was very disconcerting. The concept was nearly impossible to understand but now I had something to work with.

Whether it was on my time or it happened when it was supposed to, I don't know. The person that needed full time care and attention was me, something I never really gave much thought to. I would have to trust that there was nothing wrong with wanting to know the truth and I certainly deserved it.

33

Grave Secrets

Two days after Christmas 2017, I received a condolence call from Aunt Gloria. She had just heard from her son that Mom had passed away. Mom had been dead for more than 36 hours, yet no one had called to tell me. She had apparently fallen and hit her head. She was seen at the hospital only to be discharged to fall again several days later. The second fall proved grim, leaving her clinging to life by means of a ventilator. Jack made the decision to remove the life support and made no efforts to consult with me on this end-of-life decision.

After her death, Jack called Aunt Bert and her son, who told another cousin, who told Aunt Gloria, who then called me. It was fourth-hand news. Even after all the years of being overlooked and undervalued, I still felt a flicker of surprise that even Jack neglected to include me in this process. He claimed he wasn't able to inform anyone of Mom's death because he was too distraught – "he had lost his mother".

Less than an hour after I heard the news, I got a call from Mom's life insurance company asking me what I would like to do with the insurance money.

"Do you want to put it in trust or do you want a check?" they asked. I didn't know; I never expected to be on the life insurance policy, nor did I have time to process the news of Mom's death.

"You will need to decide so we can set up the trust or send you a check," the agent informed me. It was all too much, my brain was on overload, I didn't have any idea how to answer these kinds of questions so soon after the news, and how had they contacted me so quickly after her death? Trying to catch my thoughts I asked, "How much is it?"

"Well, you need to pay for the funeral first, and then we will split the rest with the other beneficiary, your brother," she continued. "I would say approximately five hundred dollars total."

I was stunned and couldn't help but chuckle through my grief; I was living in a poorly written satirical comedy. "You are asking me if I want to put two hundred and fifty dollars in a trust?"

Apparently, Mom's boyfriend called the insurance company immediately after her passing, hence their promptness. There was enough time for him to call the insurance company, yet it took four different family members before a call the daughter of the deceased.

Although I was still listed in the insurance policy, Mom had taken the opportunity to write me out of her will. She had also changed her prewritten obituary to leave out any mention of me or my family. I wasn't put out by the loss of my place in her will, as I didn't want anything she had to give. But this was her last slap, her last word from the grave. She wanted that last "gotcha!", leaving a reminder that she was and always will be in control, even after death.

The obituary listed Jack, his wife Helen, her children and grandchildren, and Mom's "second family," Julia, her husband and grown children. Also listed was one sister Bert, her boyfriend, Mick, her new girlfriend, Sue Ellen and her dog. Missing was her other sister Gloria, me, my husband, and all my children and her only grandchildren.

The obituary opened up floodgates for endless emails and phone calls offering condolences; not for her death but for her lack of class and empathy, as she spewed forth her mean streak towards me from beyond the grave. No one was surprised, just sad that it could go as far as it did.

Losing a parent is indescribable, and even more difficult when you had a relationship that was estranged. For me, the emotional distance between us added a few extra levels of loss I had to cope with. I was overwhelmed with feelings of grief, thoughts of what could have been, and questioning whether I even had the right to grieve. There were times when I felt relief that she was finally gone, but this only made my guilt more visceral. To complicate the matter, any chance I had to salvage this damaged relationship was gone, and she took the answers to my unasked questions with her. We always think we have more time, right up until the very second time runs out. It is at that moment we experience the magnitude of our loss.

Cari, the funeral home office manager, called me a couple of weeks after Mom's passing. She wanted to know why I hadn't signed the paperwork releasing the insurance money for the funeral. "I didn't know I had to," I replied. "The agent didn't mention anything about it."

A call that should have taken one minute lasted a full hour. After clearing up the paperwork, Cari asked me if Mom and I had been estranged, and was curious as to the nature of our relationship. Cari's husband Erik had been a classmate of Jack's, so they knew I existed and were curious as to my absence from the obituary.

After giving her a short explanation, she in turn unburdened herself from her experiences with my mother spanning over the course of several years. Her story began with the ways in which my mother acted towards Cari's husband, Erik. Mom was prone to making sexual advances toward him, dropping innuendos, and telling him that as the mortician, he would be "the last person to lay her". This was actually a "joke" I had heard her make repeatedly over the years. Cari went on to say that Marilyn told stories of an encounter (of a sexual nature) she had in a barn with Erik's father, and asked them to remind the father that "he was no angel".

I listened with the all-too-familiar disbelief I had come to associate with the infamous stories of Mom's behavior. It amazed me that these tales could still circulate, even after she was dead and gone.

34
Finding Cindy

In the spring of 2019, I received an email from Ancestry.com that I had a new match. It was a common notification to receive, which generally revealed a distant cousin ranging somewhere between four and five degrees of separation and usually on my mother's side of the family. I didn't expect this notification would be any different but I logged on to investigate nonetheless.

This time, something was different. This new relative fell under the category of "close relative" and the centiMorgan (cM), units measuring the amount of DNA one shares with another, had my attention. I suddenly felt like Sacagawea on a Lewis and Clark mission, eager to discover new territory. It was exciting but scary. Facing the unknown wasn't exactly comfortable, but certainly necessary.

Ancestry rated this match closer than a first cousin, but not as close as my children, and fell in a category equivalent to my brother, Jack. I clicked the link: her name was Cindy.

As if that information wasn't enough to push me off the edge of my seat, Ancestry revealed more. Colleen, a new first cousin, also appeared and was listed as the manager of both her and Cindy's account. After years of wondering, years of waiting for answers, many I didn't even know I had, with one click of a button I sent a request to connect.

Within hours, Colleen messaged me back. She was Cindy's daughter, and we began comparing notes through emails trying to narrow down the source of our DNA connection.

After a lot of digging, it seemed extremely plausible that Cindy, two years my senior, was most likely my half-sister on my paternal side.

With cautious optimism, we began sharing stories over email and Facebook. There were no clues to help us. Our mothers didn't know each other, as they grew up in the 1930's and 1940's in different states with neither mothers traveling far from their homes.

Cindy lived just a couple of towns from me but had grown up in Massachusetts, moving to Maine as an adult.

Though she knew who her biological father was, she had never met him. Her stepdad had raised her, but now both her parents were deceased. Cindy was exploring her paternal medical history and hoped to find it through a relative on Ancestry.com.

She only had a name belonging to her mother's first husband. The mystery man was Arthur Andersen. It wasn't a lot to go on, but it was a start and opened up a whole new door to my research.

Cindy's mother, Charlotte, was a kind, loving, quiet woman with solid family values. She married Arthur when she was young and lived in an apartment with her husband and younger sister. Arthur was a local amateur boxer in South Boston who worked at various odd jobs. They divorced when Charlotte was pregnant with Cindy and as far as she knew, Arthur was never seen again. Cindy accepted his absence, even as a child, and grew up contentedly with her mother and stepfather. Charlotte died young, passing away from an embolism in 1982, never confiding in Cindy or any of her relatives.

We worked together and within a day found Arthur's obituary and located his three children—two living, his youngest son Sonny, daughter Donna and one deceased, Arthur Jr.

With a random telephone number found on the internet, I texted Sonny, with a simple, "Hi I am Deb Landry. I am looking for one of the children of Arthur Andersen Sr. We are linked on Ancestry.com and I would like to know how we are related. I have sent you a friend request on Facebook and am wondering if you are willing to talk to me. Thank you".

Within minutes, Sonny replied, "I've always known about you and didn't know how to find you, how old are you?"

I was excited, but it wasn't me that he was looking for. "It is my half-sister you are probably referring to. Her mother was married to your father. How did you know about her?" I asked.

"Our family pictures always contained a photo of another baby that I didn't know. I asked Mom several times who the baby was, when one day she finally told me, 'Your dad had a baby girl that was born before he and I married.'

(referring to Cindy)." He said, "She must be the one in the picture."

"Picture? You have photos?" I asked enthusiastically. "My mother was from Maine, was your father ever in Central Maine?" We both had so many questions, and we couldn't get them out fast enough.

"I don't know if he was ever in Maine," he said. "I'm 59, my sister Donna is 65, she's the oldest, and my brother Arthur Jr died two years ago. You know, Dad died over ten years ago." *(Cindy was 66 at the time and I was 64).*

"If it wasn't so late I would call you. Can we talk tomorrow?" Sonny asked. It was the phone call I had been waiting years for, yet somehow the few hours that passed between our two conversations from text to talk felt like the longest. Maybe it was the excitement, maybe it was a spinning mind that created more questions by the second, or maybe it was simply the confirmation of something I had suspected all along. Either way, I'm not sure I slept a wink. Sonny called the next morning and we talked for a very long time, getting to know each other.

We compared baby photos and the story of how his mother kept the worn vintage picture, marked "Cindy" in the corner, in her checkbook next to the rocking chair where she sat each day watching her soap operas, even after Arthur's death. She had kept it there for sixty-seven years, not amongst photos of her own children or grandchildren, but alone with the checks. It served as a reminder every time she purchased groceries or paid a bill. We wondered why it was kept in a special place, if it was pain or guilt, something we will never know. For whatever reason, Cindy was always on the forefront of Arthur's wife's mind.

Sonny explained that they moved multiple times throughout his childhood, attending a different school each year, later ending up in Florida.

Arthur walked away from his first marriage, from any financial responsibility, and from his unborn child, keeping only the solitary black and white photo of Cindy as an infant, given to him by Charlotte shortly after she was born.

Sonny's friendly disposition was refreshing. He excitedly welcomed the addition of not only one half-sister, Cindy, but another, me.

Together the three of us started comparing notes, family histories, vacations, and ancestors we had in common. We were able to trace Arthur's travels to a cabin in Maine, where he and his family visited every summer. It was only twenty miles from the infamous Bar L. The proximity gave us hope we would find the answers we were looking for. The combined efforts of the three of us were comforting for a while. I even visited Sonny and his husband in Orlando when I was attending a conference.

Sonny sent us a copy of the photo his mother kept of the mystery baby, and Cindy confirmed that it was her. We even compared our three baby pictures to see if there were any resemblances.

Just before we found Sonny, Cindy and I decided to take a DNA test from 23andMe to further confirm our connection. Sonny jumped on board and submitted his DNA.

Three weeks later, Cindy and I had our results: we were definitely half-sisters! I had gained a sister and a niece, two things I never expected to have. It was the best news, and my feelings were all over the place. Even after preparing myself for the possibility, I was astonished. I couldn't help wondering if Cindy was going to be as excited as I was. Did she have room in her life for a sister, and did she want a relationship?

Cindy, Colleen and I set up a time to meet. Living just 15-20 miles apart we chose a neutral location in Kennebunk at the library. Cindy's birthday was coming up and I wanted to bring her a card. I stood in front of the sister section of the card rack and realized not one card seemed appropriate. We never experienced any of the memories that the cards talked about, so I bought her a plant instead.

The meeting was like a blind date. I didn't know what to expect, what to say or if we were going to like each other. I was cautious, nervous, and excited all at the same time. What if she didn't like me, what if she didn't want to have a relationship? We met, we hugged, we talked and we both decided to open our hearts to a relationship. It was perfect. I've never had a sister and Cindy had never had a sibling. Colleen never had cousins on her mother's side nor had my children. It was all new to us. Cindy told me about her childhood. She, like her mother, was sweet, family focused and quiet. As an only child, she held many happy memories, and was the apple of her mother's eye. Her upbringing was entirely different from mine.

Sonny didn't know much about his family lineage. It was something that was never discussed in his family so we didn't know if he was Italian or not. He remembered something about a Swedish descent but that was all he knew. Cindy nor I showed any Scandinavian in our ancestry, so we figured it came from Sonny's mother's side of the family.

It seemed like the search was over. We found the man Charlotte named as Cindy's biological father and the journey would leave us building a happy new family, but when Sonny's results arrived, the story took a detour. He was not related to me or Cindy. I called him to break the news. It broke my heart to tell him; I knew what it was like to search for answers and not be able to find them. I knew the pain of hopes built up only to fall short, but I also knew that the news would be best delivered from someone who understood. Besides, even if we ended up not being family, we had still become friends, and truth was what we all were searching for. He was so upset, understandably, and we were all left in limbo. Cindy and I left somewhat empty-handed, not knowing who our Dad was, and Sonny left realizing he never had a half-sister to begin with.

What we found even more sad is another secret that unfolded in Cindy's paternity. Did Arthur know? Did Charlotte know? Is this what broke up their marriage or was the marriage already falling apart when Charlotte became pregnant? We assumed Arthur lived his life in limbo, wondering if he was the father or if it was another man his wife had an affair with. We know Sonny's mother held strong feelings for this secret, as she continued to keep Cindy's picture. Either way, Arthur never took any role as a father to Cindy, he walked away. We will never know what happened. It just led to speculation as we continued to investigate our joint paternity further, and led to another mystery. No living members in Cindy's family had information on Charlotte's relationship with anyone else or about her divorce and first marriage. Cindy concluded that her mother must have had an affair. We just had to find him.

35

Family Trees

Discouraged to say the least, all Cindy and I could do was wait for another match to show up on Ancestry or 23andMe. Although we allowed a brief period of self-pity for our bad luck, we were soon back to researching with our usual optimism. The best part was we had each other.

It wasn't long before we had a new match for a second cousin on 23andMe, which gave us a clue that Cindy and I probably shared great-grandparents. I emailed the new cousin asking if he had any information – his name was Tomas DeLuca.

Now we were on to something, Cindy and I thought. Tomas responded immediately. He was more than willing to answer my questions, so I sent him an email with my many inquiries: Who are your uncles, how many do you have, what is your grandmother's name, etc. I don't think he was expecting the laundry list of questions I sent, and the majority of his responses were "I don't know", but he said he would ask his sister, Lynn, for clarification.

Lynn DeLuca Winters, a retired nurse, was a match with us on Ancestry.com as a possible third cousin. She was, and still is, an incredible source of comfort and information and through and through an amazing person. She proved to be an invaluable asset to our research. Over the following weeks, she would call as she remembered various family gatherings, weddings, names of distant relatives, and would send copies of her parent's letters, address books, and diary entries for us to sift through.

Again, as with Sonny, I was on the phone with Lynn for hours, making charts and family trees in the effort to bridge the gap. This time, I was even more optimistic. We had known there was a blood relation between us and the DeLucas, even before making contact. The likelihood of sharing great-grandparents was reasonable, and now it was just a matter of pinpointing which uncle or cousin was our biological father.

As summer approached, Cindy and I began building our family tree, starting with the DeLuca family. Lynn, Tomas, Angela (another cousin), Lynn's daughter Susan, Cindy, and I, planned to meet at Lynn's house where we could go through photo albums, documents, and our family trees.

What began as a solo journey of discovery had grown into a conglomeration of truth seekers, a whole group of people looking to find this one man. At this point, Lynn, Cindy, and I were convinced that we were DeLuca's. Cindy and I fell in love with the family name, the new relatives, the stories, and we had high hopes that we would find our biological father within the history of the DeLuca family.

During our search we found two uncles, both deceased, and two possibilities on the DeLuca side of the family. If we shared the same grandfather, then it had to be one of these men, or possibly an unknown man fathered by Grandfather DeLuca.

Luis, the younger uncle, had four grown children a few years younger than Cindy and I. They were all professionals living in the area, each having attended college and holding prestigious jobs. The second uncle, Daniel, never married and worked in a local mill from the time he graduated high school until he died. He lived alone, and rode a bike everywhere he went. He never drove, was a recluse, and had no children. Although this didn't prove one way or another that he could have been our father, we were nevertheless certain he had never been to Maine, and I was almost 100% positive my mother had never left the state until her honeymoon, after I was conceived.

Seeing Luis as a possible resource, I reached out to his four children through email, explaining that we were searching for our biological father and had a hunch it may be their uncle, Daniel. We explained our connection to Tomas, Lynn, and Angela, and sent them confirmation of the test results to alleviate any doubt.

Throughout this entire process, I kept in mind how strange and uneasy it must be to receive an email out of the blue from a total stranger claiming to be a distant relative. Anticipating some apprehensive reactions, I always included a link to my website and some personal information so that they could verify my identity and credentials. Nevertheless, this didn't yield my desired results and set me up for rejection. Of the four siblings I contacted, two refused to talk with us and the other two said they weren't interested in helping, and didn't want to know if there was a connection between our families. It was yet again, an emotional dead end.

One day over lunch with Lynn and our other newly found cousins, we skimmed through her mother's family records and photos. Under her breath Lynn whispered to herself, "Well, there was that Romano son…but it couldn't be him, he was too young. What a creep….". Trailing off, she said nothing more about the Romano family.

The enormously tedious maze was irritating and extremely frustrating. We were on a rollercoaster of high hopes and disappointments, the trajectory beginning to parallel some sort of mental breakdown or episode – something I was all too familiar with. The more elevated the findings were, the more profound the disappointment was when we plummeted to another dead end. Although I had been reluctant to hire an expert to help, I changed my mind when Lynn sent me the link to a CBS This Morning segment about an 18-year-old genealogical whiz kid. He was hugely successful in linking families together with DNA, and finding him to be reasonably priced, I hired him to help.

I had to wait a couple of months. The recognition he received on his national TV segment inundated him with work. While I waited, I continued the search on my own, and when he finally did get to my case, he couldn't present any results I hadn't already discovered. He was gracious and kind, and refunded half of his fee amount due to his inability to help. He concluded that the only way we would find our father is if a new match showed up on Ancestry.com or 23andMe.

I was now five years and five months into the journey of finding my biological father, and the majority of the discoveries had occurred in the last 5 months. Finding Cindy, meeting Sonny and Lynn, had all happened recently.

The weekend following the news from the young genealogy expert, Cindy and I planned a weekend gathering – an opportunity for our families to finally meet. Although Cindy and I had spent months talking and getting to know each other, our families had never met – and we felt it was high time.

I spent the whole weekend preparing for the Sunday barbecue, excitedly cooking, shopping and planning—from the red buffalo plaid linen tablecloths, to the charcuterie that lay on a bed of rhododendron leaves. I was as eager as a child anticipating the arrival of Santa Claus.

The gathering went so smoothly it was as if it was a dream, and Cindy's family was as warm and welcoming as her. Two families, finally meeting, sharing in the excitement and love and gratitude Cindy and I had experienced in finding each other only a few months before in the

Kennebunk Library. Not even some discouraging news from an expert could put a damper on our weekend.

After the barbecue, Cindy and I discussed our next move. We considered everything from psychics and more tests, crossing our fingers and waiting for another match online, to hiring yet another expert. We settled on researching more sites on the internet, while also crossing our fingers for more matches. As the old cliché goes, when God closes a door, He opens a window. Our story was no different.

Two days after our family gathering, we received an email from 23andMe notifying us of a first cousin match. The cousin, Kelly Armand, was not related to Lynn, Tomas, or Angela. This meant Kelly would be related to our grandmother's side of the family. The DeLuca's grandfather and our new cousin shared great grandparents and his grandmother was a sister to the DeLuca's grandfather.

Being novices, Cindy and I never investigated the maternal side of our biological father's family, leaving off 50% of the possibilities. The DeLuca family gave us so many prospects we never thought to simultaneously focus on our Grandmother Romano's side of the family.

Kelly's DNA profile listed him as Western Asia, Iranian and Italian. Being a confirmed match, we were able to conclude that neither Daniel nor Luis could be our father, and he would have to be a descendant from the Romano side.

I wasted no time in emailing my new cousin, Kelly. Within hours he responded and was willing to talk. Kelly was overflowing with information, hope and stories. He held the key that finally unlocked the nearly seventy years of secrets. He immediately detected the mysterious patriarch by methodically listing all his uncles and cousins, then eliminated them by age and ancestry. He had already surmised who the culprit would be, but needed to confirm it with some answers to his questions.

Kelly's mother, Anna Minoli, was the youngest of seven. Kelly was convinced that my grandmother had to be Anna's eldest sister, Maria Minoli. Maria married Antonio Romano, the brother of Lynn's grandmother. This was the connection between the Minoli's and DeLuca's, related by marriage. My great grandmother was a DeLuca.

Maria and Antonio had two sons, Nicky and Alberto. Remember Lynn saying that there was a creepy guy? That was Nicky. He had an older brother, fifteen years his senior, whom she had entirely forgotten.

Kelly, a few years younger than me, referred to his first cousin as "Uncle Al", who clearly stood out as the one we were seeking. In fact, based on the ancestry connection between Lynn and Kelly, "Uncle Al" was really the only option. He would have been more than 20 years older than Kelly, and we were confused as to why Kelly showed up as a first cousin on DNA match. We concluded that Kelly must be our first cousin, once removed.

Kelly told me many stories about his cousin, who always wore dark sunglasses and drove around in black Cadillacs. "He was cool, yet scary," he confided. "He had a way with people and knew how to get what he wanted," Kelly said nonchalantly.

One story he told about his "Uncle Al" was a rumor that he had a mistress. "He always had a mistress," Kelly said. As a young boy, Kelly didn't know what the word mistress meant. He remembered hearing the adults talking about it, but as far as he was concerned a mistress could have been a car or some other type of possession. "Alberto was a player and loved the women, he always had mistresses and girlfriends," one family member told Kelly. "He was not a gangster, but he acted like one and was heavily involved in betting and gaming, a con man." This helped us connect the dots between Alberto and Arthur Anderson, the man Cindy knew as her biological father. Arthur's amateur boxing must have connected Cindy's mother Charlotte to Alberto at boxing matches where he would place bets.

Now I had a real lead. Within seconds I had an obituary and names of three possible half siblings. I called Cindy immediately after talking to Kelly and we began our plan to contact the potential siblings. This time it was different; we had filled in every blank in our family tree except for our biological father, probably Alberto, who we now knew to be a traveling salesman in New England. In addition, I was able to place him in the Bangor, Maine area during the time of my conception—fifteen miles from the Bar L Ranch.

Layer by layer we were getting to the identity of the unidentified sperm donor. We could hardly believe our luck. It was hard not to get our hopes up every time something like this happened, but we could feel this time was different. Obtaining their contact information through public records, I wrote a letter to each of our possible siblings: Amy, Antonio and David, being sure to attach documents and web addresses to our DNA test findings.

These letters were sent via priority mail, and a fourth one to Nicky, Alberto's younger brother, who was still alive and a retired policeman in NYC.

Addressing each person individually I wrote:

September 22-24, 2019

Dear Amy:
I'm really not sure how to start a letter like this, and I apologize for the intrusion on your privacy. I will try to explain as simply as possible and want you to know, I got your name from Kelly Armand, internet research, and your address from Lynn DeLuca.

I am writing on behalf of my sister, Cindy Thibodeau, and myself. After a long 5-year search, I found out a few months ago that I have a half-sister, who is Cindy. Until that DNA test, Cindy thought another man was her biological father, a man she never met. Although we live in Maine, Cindy's family is from Massachusetts.

Recently Lynn, her brother Tomas, Kelly, and I found out we are all cousins on 23andMe. They, along with a professional in DNA and genealogy, have been helping Cindy and I find our biological father. The expert tells us that our father is a possible first cousin of Tomas DeLuca Sr., who was Lynn and Tomas' father. We have built our paternal family tree based on the DNA relatives we have connected with and found that our father was either a DeLuca or Minoli. Our theory, based on age and timelines we've uncovered, is that Antonio Romano and Maria Minoli may be our grandparents. That means that you and I may be related, even as closely as first cousins or possibly half-siblings.

With the connection to Kelly, we know that we are probably not a DeLuca cousin and more likely a Minoli cousin. From our research, the only person it can be is either Alberto Romano or an unknown male child conceived by Maria and Antonio Romano. (Not them separately, because then Kelly would not be our relative, and DNA tests confirm he is).

If your father is our biological father, we were conceived when he was a young man, possibly before he was married to your mother, I assume, as I am 65 and Cindy is 67, which means we were conceived in 1951 and 53.

We would like to talk with you about this and see if we can test this theory. The only way to do so is to compare our

DNA to one of the grandchildren of Maria and Antonio. I am writing to ask if you would consider speaking with us, or possibly taking a 23andMe DNA test so we can see how we are related.

The amount of shared DNA between us, if any, would tell us whether our theory of the relationship is correct or not. I would supply the test for you from 23andMe, would process it and pay for the test if necessary.

I know this may be out of the blue and shocking, much as it was for us to find out that our fathers of over 60 years were not biological. We will respect whatever you choose, but hope you will help us in our journey to confirm our biological father.

We want nothing more than closure and family history after a 5-year-long journey, we are not after anything else. We are most interested in family medical history, and would never intrude on your family if that is your wish.

If you would like to talk on the phone or in person, we are open to that and would meet at your convenience. I have listed contact information and you can check me out on my website, Facebook, etc., so that you can see that we are real people. I have also enclosed the family tree and confirmation photos from 23andMe.

Thank you for your consideration and for taking time to read our request. Again, I apologize for the letter, we really

didn't know exactly the best way to contact you. I did send a similar email to your brothers and uncle.
We look forward to talking with you,

Sincerely,
Deb Landry

Dear Deb,

I have received your letter today and was aware of the email you sent to my brother David. Our feelings on this is somewhat unknown since neither of us have ever thought about taking a DNA test. I understand your need to find answers, but our father has passed away and our mother is 90 years old, and we of course want to protect both of them. A DNA test is not something my brother is willing to do at this time, or anytime in the future. I will consider being tested, but first I have a few questions and noticed something on your DNA test that doesn't make sense in us being half siblings.

Your DNA shows Kelly as your first cousin? If that is true Kelly and my father were first cousins. Have you done more research into the Minoli side? My grandmother had two brothers-they were not married, that I know of, when you and Cindy were born.

I would like to know about both your mothers, like where they grew up and how your mothers could have known my father? Was there information either mother gave over the years?

If you could clarify some of these things then we can go from there. If I decide to do this, I will get my DNA test on my own and will get my results and possibly share from there. I hope we can keep this amount of communication to ourselves. I realize there is more family you could reach out to but again my mother is my main concern moving forward.

Amy

Dear Amy,

Thank you so much for getting back to me, I had no idea of the right way to contact you and knew any way was going to be a shock and upsetting. Needless to say, it has been difficult reaching out to people, researching and trying to figure what happened so long ago.

Let me see if I can clarify the paperwork and answer your question, but first I want to address your mother.

We totally understand and respect your feelings. Cindy and I will respect her and your privacy, she need not know anything. You have my word we will not disrupt her or your lives if it turns out we are siblings. I know you don't know us, but you do have our promise that we are not out to make any trouble.

Kelly is our first cousin once removed in DNA terms, or second cousin, he is not a first cousin. Meaning his first cousin is our biological father. So, the biological father is a first cousin of Kevin and a first cousin, on the other side, of Tomas DeLuca, Sr.

We are also not saying Alberto is 100% our biological father. He is the most likely person, but there could be another person, a child no one knew about maybe?

Here's what I know about a possible meeting of both women to the biological father. I don't know if your parents were married in 1950 or 1953, but I do know that both pregnancies were unknown to the biological father and neither woman ever told him or anyone the truth of paternity. Also, our mothers did not know each other to our knowledge and lived hours apart in different states.

Cindy's mom was married, but got a divorce while still pregnant with Cindy. The man who was supposedly Cindy's father had another son later on, who we contacted and found shares no relation to Cindy. So, Cindy just found out that the man her mother had been married to, and claimed had fathered her child, in fact had not. Cindy's mom passed away as a young woman and is buried in the same cemetery as your father. She did the DNA test in March because she needed family history for a medical condition and that was when she connected to me as a "close relative" on

Ancestry.com. We decided to do 23andMe and it confirmed we were half siblings. Both of us were very surprised to find out we are half Italian.

My story is very different, all I know is that my biological father was a very handsome Italian man not from our area. My mother lived in Newport, Maine. Based on stories from my aunts, my mother was friends with a young Italian man who came to the Bangor area for business.

To both Cindy and I, the only goal is the truth. We aren't looking for a new family, or to create trouble. The people who raised us are our parents, we aren't looking to change that.

I hope this helps you understand the situation and the possibility for how our parents could have met. I appreciate you responding and being open to helping us, more than you know.

Let me know if you have any other questions. I am sincerely grateful for your time and response.

Sincerely, Deb

Dear Deb,

Thank you for answering so many questions and I can't imagine finding these things out so much later in life. I can find out the names of great grandparents. I ironically was just starting ancestry because I'm hoping to travel to Italy in the next couple years and wanted to explore where my family was from. I do know my grandparents came here around 17/18 years old, of course through an arranged marriage—like most those days.

I have the DNA test and will go ahead take it so we can all have closure. My Dad was a great guy and if he ever knew he had other children I know he would have done whatever was needed.

I will plan to send DNA this week and we can go from there.

Regards Amy

After this correspondence that happened over a two-day period, Amy emailed me back saying she had a 23andMe test in hand and was sending it in. We had what I thought was a nice conversation, and she told me some stories about her family. She told me her father passed away of a heart condition seventeen years ago, six months after his mother Maria passed away at the age of ninety-three and I was able to get some medical information for Cindy. Ironically her test returned in less than two weeks, telling us she had probably sent it in long before she received our letter.

In the end, Amy was a match as our half-sister.

Upon the return of her test, things seemed to change drastically. Amy, Antonio and David, the trifecta of half siblings, were not interested in knowing or even talking to us. Amy lashed out in anger and in no uncertain terms told us the pain we had caused her. It was cold to say the least, and strangely combative. Amy demanded she would decide who would know what about her family and that Cindy and I were not allowed to speak to anyone without her permission. Our new half-sister continued, that she didn't appreciate us pressuring her family and digging up things her father did in his twenties. Reaching out to *their* family had now opened up a journey they weren't expecting.

We heard their pain, knowing all too well how it felt to be slapped with someone else's past indiscretions. The truth was staring all of us in the face and although Cindy and I had been preparing ourselves for weeks, the Romano trio wasn't ready for it.

Finally grasping this new reality was surreal. Alberto fathered five of us, that we know of, and his marriage to Izabel, mother of the trio, if he was actually married to her, didn't justify possession on Amy's part. Even if Alberto didn't know about Cindy and I, he was still our biological father, it was not a deposit in a sperm bank, but a conscious choice made by him and our mothers. Needless to say, we now confirmed that Alberto did have a relationship with both our mothers and we were able to complete the picture of who we were biologically.

Soon after the results came in, Amy deleted her 23andMe account. She didn't realize that her information would automatically show on all her DNA matches, or that it would inform Cindy and I that she was a match.

We have not heard from any of them since.

36

The Father

Alberto Romano was born in April of 1930 to first generation Italian immigrants. His father and uncles came to the United States through Boston harbor, and settled in the Greater Boston area in their early twenties. We were able to trace the families back to 1822 and Bari, Italy. There is no information on his early childhood growing up in the Boston suburbs, but we have traced the family throughout Norwood, Walpole, Norfolk, and Dedham, Massachusetts. As Alberto grew older, we were able to gather stories from his cousins and track him to the neighborhood of Hyde Park after he graduated from high school.

Hyde Park was also the same area frequented by Cindy's mother and her husband Arthur. Arthur the boxer and Alberto, a gambler. This is where Charlotte, Cindy's mom, probably met Alberto.

As a traveling salesman, Alberto travelled to Bangor, Maine on a regular basis. He was the man that went to my Aunt Myrna's house in North Newport looking for a room for a semi-secret tryst, after meeting my mother at the Bar L one night when she was there with her then boyfriend, my Dad. They made secret plans to meet the next day.

Alberto Romano was the oldest of four children, the only boy until he was in his late teens, when the last child Nicky was born.

Most of what we know about Alberto is what family and legal documents from our research have told us, and we have no confirmed childhood stories. We know from records and census that he worked in a factory as a candy maker and was a traveling salesman throughout New England, but we don't know what he was peddling, maybe the candy.

We are still not sure that he was even legally married to Amy's mother Izabel, as we have never been able to find a marriage certificate within the United States. However, as we were looking, we found three other marriages he had over the years. With this little information we were able to build a timeline of Alberto's life through marriage certificates, year books, Ancestry.com and court records.

Alberto was married three times in three different towns in New Hampshire. In 1950, at age 20, he married Angela Z. in Portsmouth, New Hampshire. The marriage license states it was his first marriage, and states that he was a self-employed traveling salesman.

In September 1951, Alberto had a brief relationship with Charlotte, Cindy's mother, resulting in her birth in July of 1952. Two years later in September 1953, Alberto was in Bangor where his affair with my mother resulted in my birth in July of 1954.

One month before my birth, in 1954, Alberto was again married, this time to a Donna P. in Nashua, N.H. According to the marriage license, she was from Bangor, Maine. We can now again assume that Alberto was in Maine as a traveling salesman, possibly at a camp with Arthur Andersen, whose family spent the summer in Central Maine every year, and met up with Donna P. and my mother at some point.

This second marriage certificate gave all of his demographic information, along with correct parents and dates of birth. On the marriage certificate, this marriage was also stated as his first, and this time he listed his occupation as a candy maker.

In 1955, nine months after his second marriage, he wed Marion H. in Seabrook N.H., listing his occupation as a salesman, and claiming again that this was his first marriage. We thought at first it may have been men with the same name, but all the documented information on all three wedding certificates confirmed the correct names, address, parental information and date of birth. What was missing were records of divorce and a legal marriage certificate with Amy's mother, Izabel Romano, sometime between 1955 and 1960 when their first child was born. Of course, this doesn't mean he wasn't married to Amy's mother, but we have not been able to locate a marriage certificate from 1940 on, or any divorce decrees from any of these women. We also found court records of our Alberto Romano impersonating another Alberto Romano, trying to withdraw funds from the other Alberto Romano's bank account. This confirmed it was our father, Alberto, based on address and birthdates filed with the courts. After 1960, there were no public records and our search came to an end. We only assume this is when his life with Amy's mother began. We surmise there is an intriguing story with the four marriages, which I can't wait to investigate.

After almost six years of searching, I finally had my hands around the answer to a question of who my biological father was. Oddly anticlimactic and yet no less satisfying, I had uncovered the last secret stone my mother set upon my shoulder. I was the daughter of a narcissistic mother and polygamist, gambling con man. Something to be proud of.

Part 3

Forgiveness

To forgive is to let the prisoner free and to discover the prisoner was you.

Lewis B. Smedes

37

Independence

As we know, education is the key to success. It is knowledge that lessens our struggles and helps us make informed decisions. I have read many books, including going as far to research the DSM-5 terms, (Diagnostic and Statistical Manual of Mental Disorders, which is the publication for classifying mental disorders by professionals). From this research, I have listed some of references on my website. I want to pay homage to some of my all-time favorite books, *The Body Keeps the Score,* by Bessel van der Kolk. Dr. Van der Kolk, a Boston based psychiatrist, who has specialized in PTSD since the 1970's and *The Boy Who Was Raised as a Dog: And Other Stories from a Child Psychiatrist's Notebook-What Traumatized Children Can Teach Us About Loss, Love, and Healing* by Bruce D. Perry, M.D. Ph.D. With that said, books can never take the place of a great therapist, but can greatly add an important piece to healing.

From the DSM-5, I made a list of symptoms from the disorders to compare with the symptoms Mom exhibited. I focused on Cluster B because most books and experts referenced this particular section. I found that Cluster B consists of Borderline Personality Disorder (BPD), Narcissistic Personality Disorder (NPD), Histrionic Personality Disorder (HPD), and Antisocial Personality Disorder (ASPD, or sociopathy). I, of course, did not get the answer or diagnosis I wanted, but read that a person needs to demonstrate at least five of the listed symptoms to be diagnosed. Interestingly enough, had Mom been diagnosed I would suspect she would fall into the category of an antisocial personality disorder with borderline and histrionic traits and features. The lack of empathy, conscience, or the inability to feel guilty about having done wrong, classified her as antisocial. Mom showed signs of most of them, not one of the disorders, but all of the disorders combined. There were two I didn't have conclusive information on, and that was childhood trauma or sexual abuse and thoughts of suicide.

I have a better understanding of mental illness and antisocial disorders as a whole and the schools of thought on the causes. Antisocial has a more complex meaning for me now that wasn't there before; an unwillingness or inability to associate in a normal or friendly way with others. It is not only being shy, it is antagonistic, hostile, threatening, unfriendly, and a menace in society.

I also wondered: if I asked anyone about various mental illnesses, would they be able to explain it to me? I know I didn't have the knowledge before my investigation. When we say sociopathy and psychopathy, most people think of the television show, *Criminal Minds* or infamous psychopaths like Charles Manson, The Boston Strangler, and Ted Bundy. They are the extreme. There are many high functioning people with these incurable emotional disorders right in our own backyard; about fifteen percent in Americans and thirteen percent of individuals worldwide. My first exposure occurred in my childhood home.

Following therapy, the estrangement, discovering my paternity, and Mom's passing, there were still a few pieces of the puzzle missing and this research into mental health helped tremendously.

Moving through my journey from trauma to genetic discovery, I realized that I was not alone; many people are victimized by mentally ill parents, partners or bosses and are recuperating from the shock of a paternity secret.

Converting life-long secrets and lies into real tangible truths, I embarked on a powerful healing exercise, and in doing so, built the strength to find forgiveness. I gained a whole new outlook on life and was slowly able to come to terms with the fact that the hole created by the absence of my mother's love would never be filled. It mirrored the exclusionary behavior of a bully; I was the target, the victim, and this is a fact. The tools I used in my professional life were what I needed in my personal life. I was already working through issues without even realizing it. Blaming my mother for depriving me of comfort and love didn't allow me to move forward with my life and held me prisoner, which is right where she wanted me. In order to let go, I would have to find a way to forgive her.

The research helped, as Mom's condition was never about me at all, it never is when a narcissist is involved. I struggled with how to forgive someone who refused to acknowledge her own faults or ever apologize for her abuse. I questioned if granting forgiveness was a way of giving in all over again, but I realized that forgiveness did not mean forgetting, nor did it mean condoning, reconciling or excusing her behavior. I learned that to forgive meant to recover; to move on so not to let my past consume my future.

After processing the personal pain, I was able to step back and examine how I had been leading my life thus far. I was still living in silence. No one knew the inner me, the abused child and wounded adult, not even my children or family. It was a secret I let out only to my therapist and my husband, but not all of it, some still painful to talk about or too embarrassing to tell. Being able to talk about the past, I discovered the war was over and I was a survivor. I realized things would never, could never change, allowing me to retire from the front lines. Realizing that forgiving isn't forgetting was another turning point for me. I finally removed the fogged up rose-colored glasses and witnessed the parent-child relationship for what it truly was. I stopped making excuses and ended the silence. My days in denial came to an abrupt and welcomed end – I accepted that all the faults and shortcomings I had been accused of were no longer, and had never been, my burden to bear.

I was raised by a woman suffering from an antisocial personality disorder along with possible other mental illnesses; my childhood psychological trauma was devastating. I was a child who suffered at the hands of hidden abuse. It left me with invisible bullet wounds throughout my body. This information freed me from years of doubt, confusion, and sadness, and propelled me into a new age of self-healing and self-respect. Finally, I could see that the person needing full time attention was me. It was a concept I had never given much thought to.

It was hard for me, at first. Each wound needed specific attention to accept that there was nothing wrong with me. I wanted to live a stress-free life, voice my feelings and be in a peaceful place. I survived a chaotic childhood, found an escape and successfully raised two daughters with almost no resources or help, built a career with no formal education, left an abusive marriage, and was still able to find sincere love, and more children to complete our loving family. I faced years of the shame-blame game that destroyed my self-esteem and trust, but I was still standing. I made something of myself, all the while being told I was worthless. My new mantra was healthy relationships, strong boundaries, and self-respect above anything else.

By creating intention and thought behind each relationship I enter into, I am better able to protect myself from encountering those who may drain me or cause me hurt—like my mother and so many others had. Although I may have lost a few acquaintances and friends along this weeding-out process, I have solid and trustworthy relationships. The most important one is the one I have with myself and I am healthier because of it. The stability within relationships, the trust I have in my friends and family, and the strength I have found in myself may have been a long time coming, but well worth the wait. Even after all the abuse, I loved my mother and always said I love you when I called her, came to visit or left the house, but it was never reciprocated.

Mom never said I love you.

Afterword

When I think about that day when I was seven years old, standing in the street searching for a sense of belonging, I can still feel the penetrating desire to escape, to run, that I felt that day so long ago. At the time, I couldn't understand why I felt such a strong need to break away—but now I know why. Sixty years have given me the insight, the answers, and understanding as to what I was feeling. I still wonder how my child brain was able to formulate such mysterious thoughts. I can only conclude it was all due to undertaking a job I didn't know I applied for: the job of fulfilling the role of parent in a relationship with a psychologically and emotionally abusive mother who was a covert narcissist.

Back in the 1950's, Mom never thought there would be such a thing as DNA testing so she would never have to prove my paternity, only convince others her stories were true. She was never put on trial for the gaslighting, lies, deception, triangulation or manipulation. You could say she got away with the crimes, and eventually escaped in death. But that is not true. Once I uncovered the whole story, it was easy to see that she could never admit to, accept or let alone forgive herself for her own choices. It is sad to think that someone could punish their child for fifty years for the crime they themselves committed. As far as my paternity, it was just another secret and lie; no different from the many others she kept.

Mom paid her penance in the loss of any kind of healthy relationship with her daughter, her only grandchildren, and great-grandchildren. She lost her chance to provide and share in a favorable legacy, and she never experienced the true beauty of an unconditional loving family. Still, without empathy, she laughed in my face to the very end.

She knew what she was doing.

Only two family members remained with her to the end, Jack and her ninety-five-year-old sister, Bert. Her third person was her live-in boyfriend, Mick. All the rest of the biological family and long-time friends were gone.

She lived in fear, shame, and walked a tightrope until the day she died praying no one would ever uncover the secret, and she never changed her behaviors—she couldn't. She reflected that fear and psychological projection toward me.

We humans are all too familiar with the effectiveness of lying and keeping secrets when it comes to protecting ourselves from judgements, pain, and the ordeal of having to face rejection. Society has a long way to go to liberate people from the shame and fear that comes with any type of abuse, the knowledge to recognize the signs, and empower individuals to seek professional help, whether in the form of support, therapy, or medication.

Openly addressing and tackling these problems head-on is nothing to be ashamed of – neither is seeking help or forgiveness. Creating an understanding and environment of respect, acceptance, trust of one's self and others, and the importance of family support is what I hope to leave as my legacy.

This memoir tackles two important issues, child abuse and surprising DNA discoveries. They are both stigmas that haunt families in the form of paternity secrecy or mental illnesses and both deserve their time in the spotlight to bring awareness to society. Questions around these issues follow so many families, as the truth of paternity, adoption, and artificial insemination has created trauma and pain for thousands of people who are now well into adulthood and are only just discovering answers to questions they never knew had to be asked; all avoidable by telling the truth from the start. These issues are typically not associated, but in my case they were categorically connected.

My mother knew the truth, chose to deal with her secret by ignoring and burying it, therefore displacing her pain and anger all in one place—on me.

I've learned that forgiveness was never for my parents. They were probably living their own hell, making choices that they thought were right for them at the time, and never considering how it would influence generations to come. Mom with secrets, antisocial personality disorder and a possible undiagnosed mental illness, Dad with PTSD—complimented by a child that wasn't his, and a secret he never addressed for whatever reason. I don't wish to drag their lives and decisions underneath a microscope, nor do I intend to bless them with forgiveness and I am not making excuses for them. All in all, it is not for me to judge, let alone evaluate or criticize others, especially my parents. I am not the judge or jury. Blaming and passing judgment on others is not what I aim to accomplish in writing this memoir. I wrote this book for my own recovery, and others with similar pasts. I want people to know that abuse is not always seen, heard or reported. In most cases it is subtle and hidden, not dramatized like in books, television and movies.

Out of respect to my parents, I chose not to publish this until after they both passed, in order to not cause them unnecessary pain or to reveal secrets that did not have a place in this book. For this reason, as well as my own preservation, I chose to leave out the darker, more painful or incriminating stories and focus on day to day life. My goal was to find solace by telling the story of the childhood that was stolen from me, and how I got it back by getting it out of me and safely onto the page, so that others who relate to my history may find solace as well. If I help one person by showing them that they are not alone in their struggles, then it is a year of writing (and many more years of soul-searching) very well spent.

People handle trauma, stress, change, secrets and abuse in different ways. Finding the root of the pain can be an uncomfortable process, followed by the arduous task of healing those emotional wounds, but it is a necessary journey to recovery.

So many of my early-life choices were made by a girl just doing her best to impersonate an adult. My instincts were always right—my mind wasn't playing tricks on me in those moments when I felt shunned, ostracized, and unwanted. I knew more than I thought. Research and time has removed the veil behind which I couldn't see the reasons why. I am no longer that sad little girl, nor am I the unsuspecting prey of the spider's web. I am strong and proud of the foundation I built for my family.

Family, by the way, is not defined by blood. It is defined by love—unconditional love. This is a truth I've known since before I could even articulate my thoughts or emotions, and it is this truth that kept me sane during the years of having other's failures thrust upon me. As an unloved daughter I focused on the lack of maternal love for many years, believing I needed that love to grow, exist, and even heal. Freedom came from realizing that this was not true. The hollow place in my heart has narrowed but it will never completely disappear.

Early childhood development is the most important time in one's life. The emotional, social, and physical development of a child has a direct effect on their overall development and on the adult they will become. Understanding the need to invest in very young children is vital, maximizing their future well-being. I lived a childhood in name only, consisting of blame and abuse for an unknown sin. I don't wish to change anything, only to leave it in the past, live for today, and look forward to the future. I am thankful I was able to escape and recover. I thought I didn't know who I was, and through discovery and forgiveness I found that I am still me. The specifics are just so many tiny pieces of a puzzle that don't need to define me, only to hold me together as the strong woman I am.

I am free. Safe. Loved. A survivor.

Deb Landry is an author, certified parenting coach, podcast host, professional operational consultant, and activist for children's rights. She has authored three children's books, *Yankee Go Home, The Snapdragon Princess* co-authored with Kim Parrish and the bestselling award-winning *Sticks Stones and Stumped.* Her new children's book, *Summer's Shadow,* will be released in late 2020. Deb's other works include several interactive children's awareness plays on character education and bullying prevention.

A humanitarian and philanthropist, Landry specializes in bullying and harassment prevention and safe school climate planning. She has lobbied for legislation in the state of Maine and throughout the U.S., serving on ad hoc committees and works as an advocate for children, youth and teens who are affected by bullying, harassment or discrimination.

Deb knows first-hand how childhood trauma can psychologically affect the growth of youth and has spent over twenty years as the co-founder and Executive Director of Crossroads, a youth character education nonprofit with a focus on developmental education to raise resilient and respectful youth.

Deb lives in Maine with her husband Darrin.

Made in the USA
Monee, IL
20 October 2026

66035302R00157